GU00480548

ADVANCED TECHNIQUES IN DAY TRADING

A Complete Guide with Tricks and Strategies for High Profitability.

John N. Cameron.

© **Copyright 2021 by John N.Cameron - All rights reserved**.

This document is geared towards providing exact and reliable information in regard to the topic and issue covered.

- From a Declaration of Principles which was accepted and approved equally by a Committee of the American Bar Association and a Committee of Publishers and Associations.
In no way is it legal to reproduce, duplicate, or transmit any part of this document in either electronic means or in printed format. All rights reserved.
The information provided herein is stated to be truthful and consistent, in that any liability, in terms of inattention or otherwise, by any usage or abuse of any policies, processes, or directions contained within is the solitary and utter responsibility of the recipient reader. Under no circumstances will any legal responsibility or blame be held against the publisher for any reparation, damages, or monetary loss due to the information herein, either directly or indirectly.
Respective authors own all copyrights not held by the publisher.
The information herein is offered for informational purposes solely and is universal as so. The presentation of the information is without contract or any type of guarantee assurance.
The trademarks that are used are without any consent, and the publication of the trademark is without permission or backing by the trademark owner. All trademarks and brands within this book are for clarifying purposes only and are owned by the owners themselves, not affiliated with this document.

Table of Contents

Introduction

Why do Many Traders Fail?

With the numerous benefits that can be gained from day trading, it begs to question why most day traders fail. If the activity is as lucrative as it sounds, why do most of these traders fail? Understanding why traders fail can give you some insight into the common mistakes that make traders lose money. Accordingly, you will be better placed to trade wisely by avoiding such common pitfalls in trading. Here is a look at some of the reasons why traders fail.

Relying on Random

Let's assume we have a new trader in the market called John. John has some knowledge about the market just because he always watches the news on stock markets. However, John has never traded. Since he has some basic market knowledge, he feels that he can try out day trading. To this point, John has never sat down to write down some strategies which he could implement to trade on stocks. So, he opens an account and purchases 400 shares without thinking.

Fortunately, to his advantage, the stocks rise during his lunch hour period. After lunch, John decides to sell off his shares. His first sale earns him a $100 profit. His second attempt also earns him $100. Now, John has the feeling that indeed he is a good trader. In just a day, he has managed to earn $200.

After a careful analysis of John's situation, an experienced trader would argue that John's day trading activity could easily be short-lived. In John's example, he faces the risk of losing money if at all he gains the perception that his strategies are working. Interestingly, he might be tempted to increase his shares because he knows that he will earn a profit. It is important to understand that John's strategies are untested. Therefore, there is no guarantee that his trading activity could earn him returns over the long run.

The danger that John faces here is that he believes in his formulated and untested strategies. Consequently, he might overlook recommended trading techniques that would have helped him avoid common mistakes. In the end, when he loses money, he will be disappointed arguing that day trading is not lucrative. This is the trap that most newbies fall into. Their first luck in online trading blinds them from realizing the need for constant learning in this activity.

Abandoning Strategy

Let's assume that John learned his mistakes and corrected them in his future trades. Now, he relies on a strategy that helps him find success in day trading for about a year or two. At this point, John feels that he has found the right strategy that works for him. However, there is another problem that ensues. John realizes that his plan has led him to losses for more than six times now. He is in a huge dilemma wondering what to do since he cannot continue making losses.

So, what does John do? He decides to adopt another strategy. Regardless of the success that he enjoyed using his previous plan, John now feels that it is time to switch to another strategy. Ideally, this is a new and untested strategy that he will be adopting. One thing that you should realize here is that John is going for a strategy that is not tested. He is abandoning a strategy that has worked for about two years now. The risk here is that John could find himself where he started. He could incur more losses because he abandoned his tested strategy for an untested strategy.

Here, you should learn that randomness can lead to profits and that it can also drive a trader to incur losses. To ensure that such randomness is avoided, it is recommended for a trader to have a solid plan that they stick to. This is a plan that will define how they trade. A good plan ought to contain an entry and exit strategy. Also, the plan should stipulate a money management technique which will help a trader trade their money wisely.

Lack of Knowledge

Another major reason why most traders fail is due to a lack of adequate market knowledge. By failing to educate themselves about stock markets, they find themselves in a ditch [2]. You cannot count yourself as a trader just because you buy and sell shares. Certainly not! You have to learn how to analyze the securities which you will be buying. Your broker might not give you all the information that you need to become a good trader. So, don't assume that reading magazines and newspapers will get you the market info that you need.

A prudent trader knows the significance of working with a profitable trading plan. They understand why they must analyze stocks effectively to determine whether they are buying profitable stocks or not. More importantly, a wise trader should know of ideal strategies that they will employ to manage their finances shrewdly. Don't believe day trading myths circulating over the internet. Do your

13

homework by researching and educating yourself about stock markets.

Unfitting Mindset

We are human beings with emotions. However, being overly emotional can be dangerous in an uncertain trading environment. To become a successful trader, you need to work on your emotions. Dealing with your emotions will have a huge impact on whether you close your day with losses or profits. Hence, it is very important that you keep your emotions in check.

Rigidity to Market Changes

One thing that you can be sure of is that the markets are dynamic – that is, the market is ever-changing. There is no guarantee that a particular market will rise steadily throughout a buying period or fall steadily throughout a selling period. If this were the case, then everybody would have been traders. The best traders will always adjust to market changes. They will know when to buy and when to sell. Before jumping to purchase a particular stock, it is advisable to conduct a scenario analysis. Afterwards, you should devise strategic moves which will ensure that you make profits while lowering the chances of incurring losses.

Learning from Mistakes

You often hear people say that failing is part of succeeding. Well, this is true. Unfortunately, it stands as one of the main reasons why day traders fail. Learning by making mistakes here and there will cost a day trader a lot of money. Engaging in trial and error is what discourages most traders from every trying to put their money in stocks. Some even end up arguing that day trading is a form of gambling. To circumvent this problem, one should learn from other experienced traders. This way, you will reduce the chances of making losses. Equally, you will learn the tricks which can be utilized to take advantage of market volatility. Therefore, do not choose to learn how to trade through trial and error. You will only lose a lot of money beyond your expectations.

Unrealistic Expectations

Take a breather! Indeed, day trading is a profitable activity that can earn you a living. Nonetheless, this should not blind you from realizing that losses can also be made. You cannot get rich overnight with day trading. Day trading is a slow and gradual process that will see your money multiply. Traders fail because they try to force returns to cover for the huge losses that they have made. Having the right plan and sticking to it will help you in toning down your expectations. Deep inside, you should have it in mind that you are trading for a living. Therefore, patience is important.

Poor Money Management

The effort that you put in finding a working strategy is the same effort that you should put in managing your finances. A trader should stick to a plan that defines the amount of money that they will risk on a regular basis. The money risked should give the trader the satisfaction that it is worth the rewards they anticipate. Having enough funds set aside for the trading activity should not give one the impression that they need to splash their money on stocks. In fact, the more capital you have, the more you should try to preserve it.

The bottom line is that traders can deal with the possibilities of failing by sticking to a plan. Sticking to a trading plan will mean that you are disciplined enough to know the exact amount of money you will risk. It also implies that you will employ a buying and selling strategy that works for you. Most importantly, you will also give yourself time to learn what there is to learn about day trading.

Chapter 1: Trading Platforms

Trading platforms are technical tools created with computer software. These platforms are used for trade execution and managing open positions in the stock markets. Online platforms range from a basic screen to sophisticated and complex systems. The simple and basic trading platforms usually provide only order entry facilities, not much beyond that. Advanced trading terminals have many other facilities, such as streaming quotes, newsfeed, and charting facilities.

Day traders should consider their needs while selecting a trading platform. For example, are they at a beginner's level or professional? No need to spend money on highly sophisticated platforms, when you are just beginning your day trading career. Different trading platforms are tailored to suit different markets: such as stocks, forex, commodities, options, and futures.

Based on their features, trading platforms can be divided into two categories: commercial platforms and prop platforms. For day traders and retail investors, commercial platforms are more useful. These are easy to use and have many valuable features. On these platforms, day traders will find the news feed and technical charts good for day trading. Investors can also use research and education related tools via commercial platforms. On the other hand, prop trading platforms are more sophisticated and are customized for large brokerage houses, who wish to provide a unique trading experience to their clients.

For beginners, it is advisable to go for some basic online trading platform that provides a simple and easy-to-understand interface. At the beginning of your day trading career, it will be difficult to adjust to the market volatility and learn new things with every trade. On top of that, any complicated trading program may confuse a novice day trader and cause losses instead of providing ease of business.

Day traders should consider two factors before choosing a trading platform: its price and available features. A live data feed is a must for any good platform. At the same time, it should not cost the moon and some more. Therefore, the day trader will have to balance between the price and trading features. Going for a cheap platform may help cut costs, but it could provide delayed data which will destroy your day trading business. On the other hand, a fancy trading platform will put a hole in your pocket and confuse you during trading by its overwhelming range of features.

Those who day trade options will need different charting features than those who trade in stocks. Similarly, day traders in forex markets will need different types of trading platforms. Carefully consider what tools are available on any online platform. If that suits your requirements and budget, make a final decision to purchase it.

Some trading platforms are available only for those who have an account with a broker. Some may have high deposit rates before allowing traders to use it. It is also possible that some online trading platforms will easily give margin facility to their customers, while others may not provide it. All these things should be considered before investing in any trading platform.

Before making a choice, it will be better if you make a list of your requirements, then check that list against the features of any platform. Purchase the one that fulfills all or most of your requirements.

Day Trading Software

Many day traders use computer software for automated trading. This takes away their headache of spotting the trend and deciding the trade entry and exit points. Also, they need not spend hours on chart analysis and reading economic news to understand what will happen in stock markets. Day trading software takes care of all their time consuming and decision-making problems.

These days, trading software automatically analyzes chart signals, decide trade entry and exit points, profit booking and stop-loss levels, and execute the trade on behalf of the trader. The biggest advantage of automated trading is that it takes away the hazards of emotional trading. Not everyone can control their emotions, especially in stock markets, where fear and greed overcome day traders. Under the influence of emotions, they do not spot the right trend and make trading mistakes. This is one of the very common mistakes in day trading, and most of the day traders who suffer losses, do so because they cannot control their emotions.

21

Different types of automated trading programs are available nowadays. The simplest type of such program is standalone websites that provide trade signals for time-based subscriptions. These websites display trading charts, where real-time prices run through the session and generate intraday buy and sell signals. Day traders have to watch these signals and manually trade on their trading platform. Such programs cost little, and day traders can continue their subscription, or discontinuous it, based on how much profit they make from it.

Some brokerage firms also provide automated trading programs to their clients. These programs run only on that company's trading platform, and day traders can directly place buy and sell orders from the program.

Choosing a Suitable Broker

In the day trading business, a brokerage service will be like your business partner, which will link you with the stock exchanges and give you a platform to execute your trade. Also, this service will demand a fee from you for every executed trade. Therefore, you will have to consider many points before you choose a broker for day trading.

A high-class brokerage can create setbacks in your profit-making efforts, and a low-class brokerage may hide some low-quality features of the trading platform. Since this brokerage service will be the medium through which you will execute your day trading business; compare different services before making your choice.

The first thing to consider will be, does the broker fit your needs? If you are going to focus only on day trading, then you must choose a service where the brokerage will be affordable for you. Check its features whether they are suitable for intraday trading or not. Choosing the right broker will be the first step in investing in your trading business. Investing in the right tools and services will provide a solid foundation for trading.

Different brokers cater to different trading and investing needs. Their tools and features are also tailored according to their customers' needs. A brokerage service, which is focused on long-term investors, may not be a good fit for day traders. In day trading also, various services are tailor-made for day traders of forex markets, while some other services target day traders in commodities markets. For day trading in stocks, you will have to focus on brokers that have the most comprehensive features for stock traders.

The second most important step in choosing a broker will be its trading fees and facilities. As a day trader, you will be placing more trades every day. Therefore, low brokerage fees will suit your needs. Also, look for margin facilities for intraday traders, which will help you trade at a fraction of the original cost of trading.

Check out the broker's trading platform. Does it provide a live data feed of markets; or, is there any delay in its price feed? For a day trader, going for a trading platform with a delayed price feed will be like committing hara-kiri. Getting the right price at the right time is necessary to make correct trade decisions. Also, the broker's trading platform should have good speed and should not face connectivity problems. Check out social media forums to know what other customers of the broker say about its services.

As a beginner, it will be better to go with a simple brokerage plan that fulfills your basic day trading needs. In the initial stages, you will have to focus on learning how stock markets function, and how to trade correctly. Once you have successfully established your day trading business, and feel confident about various trading tricks, you can think of upgrading your system and going for more advanced trading platforms and charting software.

Remember, tools and services can help you only up to a limit. Your biggest trading accessory will be your knowledge and skills that will help you establish a good day trading business.

Top List

The first window is the Top List, which has six columns, with the first three columns for NASDAQ highest volume, highest gainers and highest losers. The other three columns are for listed exchanges (New York Stock Exchange or NYSE, and the NYSE American (formerly the American Stock Exchange/AMEX)). This list provides a good overview of the stocks that are in play that day, and it is being constantly updated. Not all the stocks that are on the Top List are necessarily tradeable for us day traders though. Often, many famous companies like Apple, Facebook, Bank of America, Microsoft, GE, Ford, etc. are listed because their stocks are always being heavily traded by institutions and Wall Street. Figure 2.2 below is a screenshot of my Top List window.

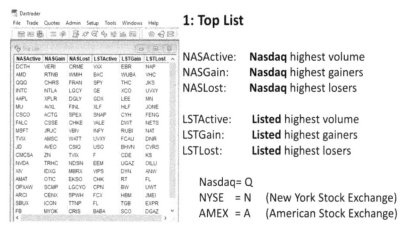

Figure 2.2 - Top List window in the DAS platform.

If instead of using DAS, you are using a different trading platform, there may be a similar window that shows the overall market activity and active stocks.

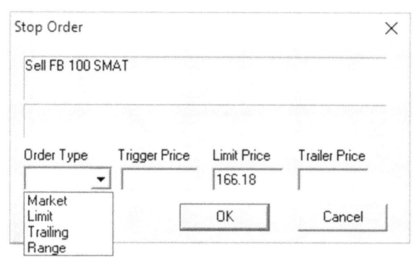

Default Style

With the Default order entry style selected, there are a limited number of fields available in the order entry area. Pressing SELL or BUY will open a new window with additional options such as order type, trigger price, limit price, etc., as set out in Figure 2.10 below.

Chapter 2: Long-term Investments and Day Trading

Day trading is characterized by the buying and selling of securities inside a single trading day. It can happen in any marketplace; however, it is generally essential in the outside trade (forex) and financial exchanges. Day traders are commonly accomplished and very much standardized. They utilize numerous trading tricks and use transient trading strategies to make monetary gains through little price changes in exceptionally liquid stocks in the market.

Day traders are receptive to occasions that cause momentary moves in the market. Trading the news is a well-known strategy. Scheduled data releases, such as financial insights, corporate profit, or loan fees, are liable to market desires and market interpretations. Hence, markets respond when those desires are not met or are surpassed, with unexpected noteworthy moves, which can profit day traders.

Day traders utilize various intraday strategies. These strategies include:

• Scalping, which endeavors to make various little benefits on little price changes for the day

• Range trading, which involves identifying a range at which a trader buys and sells at over a short period.

• News-based trading, which involves trading based on news and market expectations while taking advantage of the volatility that is associated with such news.

• High-recurrence trading (HFT) strategies that utilize refined calculations to take advantage of momentary wasteful aspects of the market.

Keep in mind that not all these strategies are suitable for every trader. For instance, a few strategies expect you to take each signal that comes along, regardless of whether you're bullish or bearish on the market.

As a new trader, you shouldn't worry about benefit objectives; however, instead, concentrate on consistency. That being stated, let's take a look at some practical benefit objectives for a profitable day trader.

Setting Realistic Profit Targets in Trading

Everything begins with defining sensible and realistic day by day objectives. Swing traders may begin with week after week objectives for evident reasons. However, as a day trader, it is imperative you set your objectives in genuine benefits, instead of pips.

It is likewise imperative to utilize a similar measure of hazard (introduction) on each exchange. Fluctuating presentation is a decent method to clear out your record – regardless of whether you're utilizing a robust trading framework.

Day by day objectives is, to a great extent, controlled by your degree of hazard resistance. For example, you chance 1% per exchange. My

30

day-by-day benefit cutoff is 2%, so you just need a couple of productive exchanges without any misfortunes to hit that mark.

If you are just gambling .5% per exchange, a progressively practical everyday benefit cutoff maybe 1% every day. It is going for 2%, while gambling .5%, and would take two to four fruitful exchanges without any misfortunes to accomplish. It's not prone to occur.

Note: Don't simply hop into the market. Gain proficiency with a decent trading framework, and afterward backtest and demo trade until you demonstrate to yourself that you can be reliable over the long haul (months or years – not days or weeks).

At the point when you begin trading a live record, utilize the littlest lot size (or the number of offers, contracts, and so forth…) accessible to you from the start. Little by little, you can increase your presentation per exchange to your ideal hazard level as you become acquainted with the mental obstacles of trading with real money.

Good traders would prescribe utilizing .5 – 1% per exchange. However, extremely propelled traders regularly hazard 3% or more per exchange. What amount of money can you afford to lose per exchange? When you have decided your degree of hazard resistance, you can decide a day-by-day objective or cutoff.

Week by week and Monthly Goals

From that point, your week by week and month to month shorts can be set. I have a progressively forceful hazard resilience, so my benefit cutoff targets are as per the following: 2% every day, 5% week after week, and 15% month to month. I don't utilize yearly shorts.

These objectives may appear to be high to certain traders, yet they are sensible for me.

Note: This doesn't imply that you make 2% consistently, 5% consistently, and so on…. If you make 2% in a day, that is a decent day of trading. Moreover, 5% is a decent seven day stretch of trading.

If you are not reliable yet, you should concentrate on learning a beneficial trading framework and turning into a long haul, reliably productive trading framework. In case you're simply beginning, going for 5% every month bodes well.

If you feel that you can double your record at regular intervals in trading, you are not prone to set reasonable benefit targets. You will probably overtrade your account to a little balance.

You will chance excessively, and you will lose excessively. Ravenousness makes traders careless and overactive in the market, which prompts botches. Little predictable and exacerbated benefits will prompt a fortune over the long haul.

Keep in mind: Money management shorts work two different ways. If you are down 2% in one day (or two misfortunes straight), stop trading that day. Quit trading if you lose 3% in a multi-week. In conclusion, use 5% as your month-to-month misfortunes cutoff. Remember that you will have a progressively forceful hazard resistance.

Advantages of Day Trading

If you want to trade stocks and you're hoping to turn into a day trader, it's critical to understand what you're getting yourself into. You need to know the advantages and disadvantages of day trading. So, if you need to change and turn into a swing trader, at any point, you'll, in any event, know the purpose for it.

Most importantly, a day trader is somebody that holds a stock or a position, not necessarily for a whole trading day, which is 6 ½ hours.

As a day trader, you can hold a position for 20 minutes, 60 minutes, or even five hours.

So, what are the advantages of being a day trader?

The first advantage is that a day trader has no medium-term hazard on holds on income since any trade is closed before the day is over. Subsequently, as a day trader, your income compounds quicker, so in case you're bringing in money every day, you're ready to utilize such money in opening other trades the following trading day.

Additionally, day trading permits you to increase your income repeatedly quickly. In fact, one of the extraordinary attractions of individuals to day trading is because it looks like making easy and quick money. Also, behind day trading, there's greater energy. Day trading keeps an individual in a regularly passionate state. In fact, tons of beginner traders are pulled into day trading because they find the fluctuation of their accounts attractive. They get addicted to the thrill of their profits going up or going down as the case may be.

If effectively managed, the benefits of day trading can far surpass the risks. However, day trading requires order and time management. Additionally, it allows a person to make their hours without a boss or manager hovering over their back. What's more, notwithstanding the measure of money an individual can make from trading from the solace of their own home, day trading offers people numerous advantages they won't experience in the more customary types of trading stocks and other monetary instruments.

The key advantages of turning into a day trader:

Similar to any industry, there is a great deal of study and information to procure before plunking down before your PC and executing your first trade. Nevertheless, an individual doesn't need to be an expert in the fields of investing. There is a great amount of free information on the Internet – and at your neighborhood library – that can help you begin your day trading profession. You can buy day trading programming (which can run you $20-30K) that can give you moment news, outlines, and stock data, however on the off chance that you are just starting, this could be an error.

Numerous sites offer people the chance to practice and learn day trading on demo programming for nothing or a little charge (nobletraders.com; thousand year's traders.com).

With day trading you work for yourself.

Simply visualize this: you are discreetly telecommuting on your PC, executing trades, while drinking your espresso, without your boss or supervisor breathing down your neck. You work for yourself. You needn't bother with demanding authorization for trades; you don't have to fulfill another person's need; you are in the game for yourself. You are dependable and responsible for your presentation. On the off chance that you fall flat, you lose money, conceivably an exceptionally huge sum. As much as we would all adoration this opportunity, it reminds you that you have to have the self-restraint and hard-working attitude to realize the business well.

36

Probably the best favorable position of day trading is the capacity to close your situation at or before the finish of the trading day. For a day trader who opens and closes his situation before the trading day closes, the risks of holding a stock medium-term are eradicated. A conventional trader's benefits can vanish medium-term with customary, long haul trading, however, with day trading, your benefits are verified as long as you close your situations before the finish of the trading day. This permits you – on the off chance that it was a decent day – to rest adequately around evening time.

No medium-term emergencies or cataclysms in the money related markets can influence your salary for that day.

Day traders can regularly exploit a battling market by using short-offering trading strategies to exploit falling stock costs. The capacity to bring in money off of the financial exchange in bearish market conditions is a huge bit of leeway for a learned day trader.

There are two sorts of examination that most traders and investors look to for monetary data: technical investigation and key investigation. Customary, long haul traders have the chance to concentrate on an organization's essentials – organization wellbeing, fiscal reports, and management data – to perceive how its stock worth will change over the long haul.

Chapter 3: Price Action and Trade Management

Before entering any trade, have a plan in place that includes a thorough knowledge of your risk/reward ratio (high probability trading creates a strategy that lowers your risk of loss and increases your chance of winning). A good strategy with a risk/reward ratio is the cornerstone of successful trading, but only if you use it consistently. This isn't as effortless as it seems, because once you start to trade your emotions enter the picture, especially if there is no stop-loss or limit loss in place before entering a trade.

When this happens the Day trader might focus on losses trying to turn them around, which is counterproductive. Better to cut your loss and move on so that you can concentrate on your wins. Planning against such an eventuality is the best countermove. A sound strategy for controlling your trade (when your feelings or emotions rise) is to trade with a risk/reward ration of, at least, 1:1.

Let me use an analogy: Let's take for instance the purchase of a new sofa where you want to get the best quality for the least amount of money. You, therefore, implement a strategy to manage your spending before going on your shopping trips. You call ahead to a couple of stores and ask each merchant what's available at your price point. From the list of merchants, you choose one and go shopping the next day. You take only enough money to make your purchase.

This stops you from overspending (based on an emotional reaction) once you "enter" the store. You had an entry point price and an exit point before you even go to the store, which ensured that you'd come out ahead.

Analysis with price action

What is the indicator saying about the strength of the current trend? Is it getting stronger or weaker?

Context of the market

Just like the weather, it's important to be aware of the market context. Is there news coming out that can change market sentiment? What time of day is it? Is the market in the lunchtime lull where trading volume is light (this equals less momentum)? The best plans can fall apart if you don't qualify and check to confirm that the route is still clear.

Rules vs. Intuition

During your training with me, there are times when it's required that you follow the rules that I advocate to the letter. That is what high probability trading is all about, rules-based trading, which I will show you. However, there may come a time when you have traded a particular stock or Forex pair so often that you know its heartbeat. This is when you can allow you intuition to guide you. You will find this intuition-based trading more applicable when you make the rules, find the trend, find a location, confirm the trade and apply the context of the day (news, time, volatility).

That, in essence, is the role of a trader, which is to find opportunities in the market by using rules and then applying the right strategy.

Common errors seen in traders when managing their portfolio:

1. Trading without a Trader's Plan

2. Trading too large a Position size for the following:

— Account size (too much risk)

— Experience level

— Risk Comfort level

3. Unprepared for a string of losses

4. Lack of Discipline

— Impatient

— Emotional maladjustments

Successful Traders develop a rules-based trading plan

1.   A Good Trade is one based upon predetermined rules/criteria

—   Regardless of the outcome

2.   The best traders trade when the odds are in their favor

—   Not just because the market is open

3.   Have the ability to distinguish between high and low-risk trades

Remember the Golden Rule of Trading

The golden rule of trading: Cut your losses and let your winners run.

How do we do this, by knowing how we handle risk. How much money can we really afford to put at risk on each trade? Define YOUR decision point where a trade is determined to be NOT working.

Steps to managing a trade

1.   Know What Type of Day it is:

—   Understanding how the market moves is critical

2.   Choose a Trading Strategy.

3.   Know Your Stop.

4.   Identify Your Target.

5.   It is desirable to trade when you have a high risk to reward ratio. The higher the ratio, the less you must be right.

6.   Every Trade is Different. Compute stops and position size for each trade to equalize risks.

Remember that defining your Edge is unique to you, and it maximizes your strengths while acknowledging your weaknesses. Therefore, copying someone else's strategy won't necessarily work for you. The ultimate goal is that you recognize your skills as a Stock Market trader while simultaneously tilting the odds in your favor, i.e., leveling the playing field by trading in a way that works for you.

The second component of our Trading Plan is trading in the direction of the trend. As our quote above implies, if you don't allow yourself to be distracted by the many pitfalls of the market, you may actually reach your target. This is especially true when you are trading with the trend. You may make a mistake by entering a trade at the wrong time, which we'll discuss later, but if you are with the trend, you can still reach your destination.

If you have ever had the lovely experience of taking greyhound to visit family friends, you may understand this analogy rather well. I grew up in Pittsburgh, PA. After graduating from high school, I went to Penn State University. Like any young boy away from home, I loved coming back home to visit my parents and friends. Although PSU was only about 1-hour ½ away from Pittsburgh, my parents were not going to make that trip. So, I often had to buy tickets from Greyhound.

I had two options when purchasing a ticket: Express or Neighborhood. The express would drive straight from Penn state to Pittsburgh taking about 2 hours. The Neighborhood line would stop at every small city in between the two destinations taking up to 5 hours.

My point? No matter which line I took, I made it to my destination. If you trade with the trend, you may not get to your target as fast as you would like, but the route or momentum of the market will eventually get you to where you want to be. This is not a 100% guaranteed, even a bus breaks down from time to time. Likewise, sometimes the trend ends. Thus, the saying, "the trend is your friend until it ends".

Chapter 4: New Trading and Advance Day Trading Strategies

Strategies are especially important to win at day trading. You will need to develop strategies that can be utilized repeatedly so that you can continuously build a profitable portfolio. Below I have included several diverse ways to incorporate strategies into your day trading program.

Having momentum is what day trading's all about. The first thing I learned when I started to trade stocks is, I learned that locating stocks that are moving in price will be how you can begin to profit. In every single day, there are stocks that will move in price by 20-30% and sometimes, even more, depending on the day. So how do you identify the stocks that are fixing to make moves that could be big? One of the biggest realizations that come from day trading is that those stocks that move 20-30% the shares will have limited technical indicators.

In order to have a momentum stock trading strategy, you will need stocks that are moving. If the stock is sideways or chopping, then it will be useless. Locating the stocks that are fixing to make a huge move is the first step. Using stock scanners to locate these is the first thing that you can do.

Momentum stocks will have a few similar things. By scanning 5,000 stocks you can ask for the criteria that are true to what you need. There should be a listing of at least 10 stocks per day. These will contain the ones that have 20-30% move. These stocks will help you make a living as a day trader.

Criteria #1 - under 100mil shares that float.

Criteria #2 – a strong daily chart.

Criteria #3 - at least 2x the volume for a volume that is high

Criteria #4 - catalysts that are fundamental such as PR, FDA announcements, Earnings, Investor activity as well as other kinds of breaking news. These stocks may also experience some momentum with a fundamental catalyst. If this happens then it is going to be called a breakout technical.

Using scanners to locate my stocks for day trading is an effective way to find the ones with the criteria you need. The scanners are more valuable as a tool that many of the new traders understand. Once the scanners pick up something, it will get alerted to that stock. Most investors will find that they need to buy this spot as well. These buyers then subsequently create spikes with the volume and subsequent results that are priced for quick sales as well as helping the stock move up. You should learn as a new trader to find an entry that shows in real-time. Scanners can give advice for copious amounts of trade alerts on a daily basis. Instead of flipping continuously through charts, I can see the charts I need in a quicker more relatable way. Every trader needs to be using the scanners to find hot stocks that will help them profit daily.

Blue flags are a wonderful way to chart patterns. This is a pattern that is seen every single day during the day trading hours. It can offer a risk of entry that is low in a strong stock. The hardest thing is that the traders have difficulty locating these patterns in the real-time. You can locate these stocks by scanning them in the scanners. If I use the surging up scanner, I can find the highest volume relative to the market. Pattern-based traders will look for all the patterns in the stocks that will support the momentum that is continued over time. Scanners will not be able to chart the patterns that they find. This is what you will need to help with. Maintain skills to justify each trade.

Bull Flags #1 Strategy

With this strategy, the first candle would be to make the high anew once the breakout happens. Now scan for the stocks and begin to squeeze up so that the green candles in the chart of the bull flag. Then the investor will wait for 2-3 candles that are red to pullback with a form. The very first candle that is green needs to make a new high once the pullback entry is at the stop that is low. This will typically show a spike in volume in the moment of the first candle that is making a high. This means that 10s of 1000s of traders are positioning themselves to take and send an order for a buy.

Flat Top Breakout #2 Strategy

This is similar to the bull flag strategy; the only difference is the pullback which is a flat top that has a resistant strong level. This will happen over a period so candles that are easy to recognize within the chart by the pattern that is obviously a flat top. This is a pattern that will form due to a big seller that has a specific level of price that can require the investors to purchase all available shares before the prices going higher for a continuous-time. This pattern can have breakouts that are explosive for the seller's short notice which is resistant forming levels which will place a stop order right above them. If the buyer takes out the level of resistance, it can be a stop order buy which will trigger the stock to shoot a very quick high and the longs can be a nice profit if it does.

Momentum Stocks and Where to Set My Stops

I tend to set a stop order that is tight when I buy momentum stocks. This stop order is placed just below the back pull that is the first. If this stop is farther away than 20 cents, then you may need to place the stop order less than 20 cents and return later for a second try. The reason for the stop at 20 cents is for the 2:1 ratio of profit loss. Lastly, I risk 20 cents due to the potential to make double. When you risk 50 or more you will need to make 1.00 to get a ratio of profit loss properly. This will make the trade justified. Try to avoid trades which would generate profits that are large for a trade that is justified. You will have a better chance of achieving a more successful trade for a stop of 20 cents and target at 40 cents vs. the 1.00 stop and the target of 2.00 profits.

Try to balance the risk across any trades made. When calculating risk, you will see an entry price at your stop for a look at the distance. If your stop is 20 cent and you want to max the risk, keep it at $500 and take it to 2500 shares (2500x.20=500)

Time of Day This Works Best

This is best used at the hours of 9:30-4 PM. The morning is one of the best times to trade. So, focus on the 9:30-11:30 time period, this does not mean that any time during the day we are not able to get a news spike that should suddenly bring about amounts of volume that is tremendous in a stock. This stock will have shown no interest early and then becomes a great candidate for the pullback first. This pullback that is first will be a bull flag. Once 11:30 AM arrives then the only trade-off that is done is the 5-minute chart. This is because the 1-minute chart has become choppy during the midday as well as a trading hour through to the afternoon.

Checklist for Entry

- Criteria entry #1

Momentum trading chart day pattern

- Criteria Entry #2

The tight stop will support the 2:1 ratio of profit loss.

- Criteria Entry #3

Volume is high, 2x or more, and associated with the catalyst. The volume getting heavier means that people tend to watch it.

- Criteria Entry #4

Under 100mil shares, the float is low, however, under the 20mil share that is ideal.

Indicators for Exits

- Indicator exits #1

Sell ½ when the target profit first hits. I risk $100 with hopes to make $200. Once the $200 is up, I sell ½. Then I adjust the stop for my price entry with the position of balance.

- Indicators Exit #2

At the point that I have not sold ½, the candle that is first to close red is the indicator for the exit. If ½ is sold, I'll hold the candle that is red until my stop breakeven has not hit.

- Indicator exit #3

The bar for extension will force me to lock at the beginning of my profits before the reversal inevitably begins. Bar extension is a candle which spikes up and then instantly places me up by $2-400 or more. When I have a spike in the stock, I get lucky and sell into it.

Analyze These Results

A successful trader will have metrics that are positive for their trades. Trading in stock is a statistical career. You will either have a return/loss that generates the statistics. By these statistics, they will be able to see if the commitment is there or profitability has potential. This can be done without looking into their P/L total. After you have finished every week you will need to analyze results that help you with your current metrics for trading, to understand the strategies needed.

The investors that are keeping a meticulous record for trades are the best because they are data-mining the records that help you understand how they can improve their trading. Using a monitoring system, you are able to follow your stats for trading and this can be a huge help when tuning your strategies into a fine plan.

There are several strategies for trading that can be used similarly to the one listed above. Below is a breakdown of each one of the trading strategies that I have found will work for day trading.

Momentum Trading

The investor jumps on the stock that has a moving price that is going up. Look for these things to use this strategy:

Prices that move in a unique and major way. Driven by earnings growth and surprise catalysts. The new launch for a drug company. Buyouts of smaller companies by larger ones.

Movement of 30-40% in the stocks.

A reduced number of shares that are outstanding can be traded faster by smaller stocks.

Tools like Stock Twits used for trading to maintain the momentum through ideas and trends with a platform for financial communications.

Chapter 5: Risk and Account Management

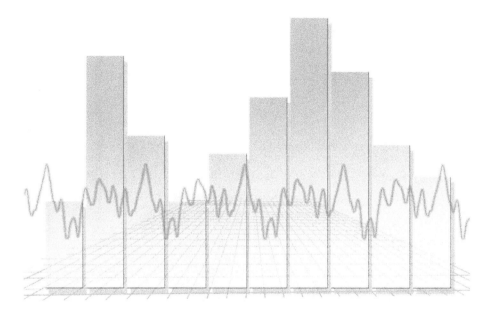

It is important that you have the right mindset when you go into day trading. It is all about your attitude. This can affect every aspect of your trades from day to day. This chapter is all about how to have the right attitude, and how to change your mindset around completely.

Trading Psychology

1. Be flexible and do not become attached to a trade. If the trade is not right, cut it loose and move on to another one.

2. Changing how you view the market day to day is the key. What you think of the market today may be a completely different story tomorrow.

3. By focusing on what you are doing now you can make quick decisive decisions. Listen to the market and forget everything you thought was being told to you by the market.

4. Gain experience and you gain intuition. By observing and experiencing the market, you will be able to gain intuition that can help you make the right choices in the market. Check the charts, the live trading streams, and maintain a log of the behavior within the market.

5. Use the strategy that is right for the idea. Start with a hypothesis and then build your strategy around that idea. Sometimes choosing the best trade is based on the underlying buy. You may find though that a currency or derivative is a better tactic to play. Seeking out the least risky trade is going to have the greatest potential for reward.

6. Draw a line that you will not cross. Before you purchase a trade find the point at which you can be proven inaccurate. Decide where your market needs to go and then examine what level you will base the idea on to invalidate the claim. This is the location to place the stop.

7. Consistency needs to be executed. Be mechanical as you can be, even if you are doing manual trades. What this means is, when I see something that meets my criteria then I will jump on it and purchase. When trading, you should not leave it up to the discrepancy of the investor's judgment. In order to win you have to toe the line and be confident in pulling triggers when necessary.

8. Embrace the risk and uncertainty of the stock market. You need to be able to see that a trade will be a loss before jumping into the trade position. Expect and accept the worse possible outcome. This will help with the focus along with the trade process.

9. Believing can be seen in the numbers. By following a direct and clear strategy you will see that the numbers will show proof of the effectiveness of the strategy.

10. Individual outcomes from trades should be ignored. Look at the collective of all the trades that you placed, not the 1 or 2 that just took place. Examine the last 20 trades and see where you won and where you lost. The outcome of an individual trade can be masked and will dilute the bias that was encountered by the investor. It can block you from repeating trades from the past that were not beneficial. This will help with future decisions that will be influenced by the bias.

The Mindset of the Day Trader

How to Start a Good Trade

You want to start a good trade off with a little bit of humility. Not counting your chickens before they hatch is a good mindset to have. However, you cannot be too negative about a trade, or else, you may jump at the first sign of increase, rather the perfect moment. It is a good idea to be confident in your trading abilities, rather than being confident in the market itself. You are the one who makes the decisions, and you control the amount of time that trade stays out there. It is good to be confident in yourself so that you are not second-guessing and missing good deals.

Mantras to Get You in the Zone

It is no secret that it is a good idea to get in the "zone" before you begin a trade. What is the zone? Well, the truth is that it differs from person to person, but the base of it is a mindset that has you focused primarily on the task at hand. You want to be able to psych yourself up for this amount of focus. The best way to do this is to look up some daily affirmations online about day trading. Affirmations are little phrases you say to yourself every day to help you lift your spirits. Choose one and make that your mantra.

How to Avoid Getting Too Cocky

Cockiness is your worst enemy. You will pump up your self-esteem too much and start to make mistakes because you feel infallible. You are not infallible. You are human, and humans make mistakes. If you go into a trade thinking that you can't make a mistake, then you are wrong. To avoid being too cocky, you should always remember that the market is volatile and that you are not magical. While you may be capable of making good decisions, you are not perfect, and the market can fluctuate beyond your control.

How to Gain Confidence

If you are not confident in yourself, you will probably second guess yourself when it comes to a good deal. You have to be confident, but not cocky. You want to be able to find that balance. The easiest way to gain confidence is to stick by every choice you make. Don't second guess yourself. You have to believe in yourself. You want to make sure that you are being confident in yourself, so you can really stick by the good decisions.

Mindsets to Avoid

Just like there are some mindsets that you should have, there are also mindsets that you should avoid. You want to avoid being too cocky. Having too much confidence can cause you to stick by predominately bad decisions. You also do not want to be too humble, because if you don't have any confidence in yourself you will probably pass up on a good deal in hopes for a better one.

How to Use a Mindset to Your Advantage

It is a good idea to have a strong mindset and to not veer from that mindset. You should go into each trade thinking that you will not settle for a bad trade. You should have the mindset that you are going to focus and watch each trade like a hawk. You want to be focused and sure of yourself, with just a hint of a realistic approach to your trades.

Why Thoughts Are Important for Success

Thoughts are essential to having a successful trade. You cannot go into a trade with a sour attitude and expect to give your trades your all. You have to leave your problems outside of the market and really focus on the trades each day. You need to make sure that you are clearing your mind every day.

How to Change Your Current State of Mind

If you wish to change your state of mind, you have to really want to have the right mindset. Affirmations as mentioned above are a great way to do so.

Chapter 6: Less Stress and More Profit

The market is a tricky place to be without the relevant information. In order to become a successful trader, one needs to understand the charts and their way of working fully.

Trading to get long term profits is called longer-term position trading. This is different from the shorter-term scalping that is day trading. If you want to head in this direction, then you must get familiar with a few strategies to employ in order to achieve success.

The most important thing you need to know is that the amount of money you inject into this venture is not going to come back in a short time and you must, therefore, be very ready to make that investment.

This then calls for a good understanding of money and a great management formula for the money. If this is overlooked, then there will be a lot of wastage, and the lack of planning also makes it hard to accumulate any profits one might gain in the venture.

Another aspect that is often overlooked is keeping tabs with the market and having a reliable market analysis daily if not as oftentimes as possible during the day. This helps in letting one know what stocks are viable and their cost, variables in its pricing, and why you should choose a certain stock for long term profits.

Trading is most beneficial when it begins and ends on the same day, as is day trading. However, when you have looked at all your options and decided to venture for long term profits, the above points are some of the considerations you should have before capitalizing on that.

Benefits of Trading

<u>Source of income</u>

Financial independence is the dream of every individual. Day trading can easily get you this freedom. A trader has the opportunity to trade as many times as they can in a single day. Depending on how well they are able to trade, they can earn huge profits from the trades that they engage in. The main trick in becoming a good investor depends on how well an investor can utilize the various option strategies to earn a source of income. For you to become an expert trader, you need to have some tactics that you can utilize. Those tactics set you apart from the novice traders. You might be wondering how you can get to this point while you are just getting started. Well, as a beginner, one of the core values you will require is the commitment to learn. Gaining knowledge makes you aware of what you are engaging in and makes it easier for you to become better at it.

<u>Flexibility</u>

We can discuss flexibility in two ways. The first way is the fact that you can trade anywhere at any preferred time and you can engage in any trade you would like.

How amazing would it be if you can earn money passively, without using much of your time and effort?

Most people do not get this, and that is why they jump into conclusions that options trading is a scam. Well, it is not as easy as it may seem. One has to use their mind and spend some time learning more about how it works. Once you get it right, it becomes easy for you. It is an investment that you can easily engage in and earn your profits at the end of the day as long as you know how to do it right. The other way is the fact that once a trader purchases an option, they have the opportunity to trade as many times as they can earn a profit.

These trades are conducted before the expiry date when the option contract is still valid. Depending on how well you utilize the option strategies, you can earn a lot.

Insurance

Options contracts can be utilized for insurance purposes. For a trader to use an option contract as insurance, they must build a good portfolio. A portfolio indicates the profits an individual has made, together with the losses. A good portfolio needs to have more profits and fewer losses. As you trade, you need to ensure that you master the art of trading options.

This involves using the right trading plan and strategies to maximize your profits. Building a good portfolio is not a hard task. It is something that you can easily accomplish as long as you are committed to what you do. You keep getting better at it with every day that passes. In the beginning, you may encounter some challenges, but do not allow them to prevent you from getting where you would like to get. It is also important for you as a beginner to trust the process and believe that you will make it at the end of it all. Once you establish a good portfolio, you can use it as your insurance. It ensures that you do not acquire a complete loss, in case a trade goes contrary to what you expected.

Cost-effective

Different options contracts are priced differently. We have some that are more expensive than others. There are several factors that we have to consider when it comes to pricing options. Some of these factors include the strike price, stock price, dividends, underlying asset, and the expiry date. When it comes to the expiry date, the options contracts that have a short period before they expire tend to have low prices. On the other hand, the options contracts, whose expiry date is quite far, tend to be highly-priced. As a beginner, you may find yourself opting to get cheaper options depending on your budget. Additionally, as a new investor, it is always good to start small. You may not be able to start with a huge investment at the beginning, especially if you have not tried it before. The beauty of investing in day trading is the fact that you can engage in any trade depending on your budget. You do not have to stretch beyond what you can afford. Any option can earn you a profit regardless of how it was priced; it all depends on your ability to earn from the options contracts.

Limited losses

The mistake most investors make is that they start trading with a lot of expectations. They think that they can make money within a short period of time, without having a strategy. I will disappoint you by telling you that it is impossible. You have to play your part in ensuring that you maximize your earnings as you minimize your losses. You cannot invest blindly and still expect an income at the end of the day. A lot of effort, commitment, and dedication will be needed. Most people miss this fact, and that is why they end up making losses. Once they have incurred the losses, they conclude that day trading is a scam. We have had a majority of the traders engage in overtrading only to end up losing every penny that they have invested. To avoid this, one has to be aware of the various option strategies. The different strategies are all aimed at increasing profits and reducing losses. This is easily achievable as long as one is committed to learning how each strategy works and when to utilize each best.

Limited risks

If you know much about investments, then you understand that most businesses, deals, or tradespeople engage in having risks. There is no single investment that an individual can engage in and fail to encounter risks. Day trading is no different from other investments. At times you will have to be open to the possibility of encountering some risks. These risks if not controlled can result in fewer profits or no profit at all. Before engaging in a trade, evaluate all the possible risks. Get to know which you can afford to minimize as you leave aside those that you have no control over. This may seem like an easy task to undertake, but you need the right option strategy to do so. Depending on the type of trade you chose to undertake, you can easily get a suitable strategy to utilize. The strategy needs to be effective in minimizing the risks so you can earn more profits. As a trader, ensure you are well aware of all the option strategies that you can utilize in a trade. This knowledge allows you to make the right decisions while trading, and you easily earn profits as you reduce the potential risks.

Make huge profits

Every investor aspires to earn profits from the investments that they make. With day trading, you can make your dreams come true. One of the good things about day trading is that you can trade multiple times. As you engage in different trades, it is good to keenly observe what you do to ensure that you avoid making wrong decisions. Ensure that you evaluate all the trades that you engage in. This allows you to evaluate the possibility of incurring a loss or a profit. You get to know the trades that you can engage in and those that you need to avoid. As a beginner, avoid the trades with a high possibility of earning a loss and at the same time have a high possibility of earning huge profits. Such trade may seem to be good, especially if you lean on the possibility of earning huge profits. However, do not forget that both possibilities are applicable, and you can also make a huge loss. In such cases, you will be required to make the right decisions that can result in you earning profits.

You can also deal with multiple trades that earn small profits and get a huge profit at the end of the day.

Less commission

Less commission means that you earn more profits. While selecting the best brokerage account to use while trading, this is one of the factors you will have to consider. Ensure that the brokerage account has fewer commissions so you can increase your income. Different accounts have different rates for their services. As you do your research, you will come across some accounts with high commissions and those with low commissions. If you go to the accounts with high commissions, it will affect your profit. You will find that a percentage of your profits will be slashed and go into catering for the high commissions. The best thing to do would be to avoid such accounts and work with those that have low commission. As a beginner, you need to properly analyze all your choices to come up with the best solution. It is a good thing that with a single click, you can get all the information you would like from the internet.

Chapter 7: Portfolio Diversification

Day traders generally execute trades in the course of a single trading day while investors buy and hold stocks for days, weeks, months, and sometimes even a couple of years. In between these two extremes are other forms of trading. These include swing trading and position trading, among others.

Swing trading is where a trader buys an interest in a commodity or stock and holds the position for a couple of days before disposing of it. Position trading, on the other hand, is where a trader buys a stake in a commodity or stock for several weeks or even several months.

73

While all these trades carry a certain element of risk, day trading carries the biggest risk.

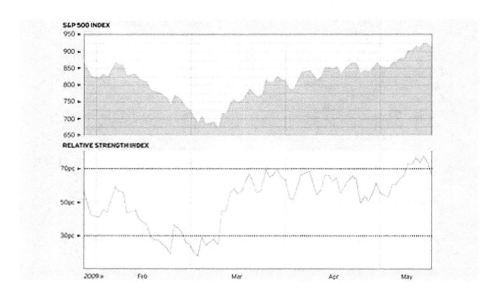

A trader with the necessary skills and access to all the important resources is bound to succeed and will encounter a steep learning curve. Professional day traders work full time, whether working for themselves or for large institutions. They often set a schedule which they always adhere to. It is never wise to be a part-time day trader, a hobby trader, or a gambler. To succeed, you have to trade on a full-time basis and be as disciplined as possible.

Introduction to Diversification

Diversification is considered an effective risk management technique. It is widely used by both traders and investors. The gist behind this approach is that investing funds in just single security is extremely risky as the entire trade could potentially go up in smoke or incur significant losses.

An ideal portfolio of securities is expected to fetch a much higher return compared to a non-diversified portfolio. This is true even when compared to the returns of lower-risk investments like bonds. Generally, diversification is advisable not only because it yields better returns but also because it offers protection against losses.

Diversification Basics

Traders and investors put their funds in securities at the securities markets. One of the dangers of investing in the markets is that traders are likely to hold onto only one or two stocks at a time. This is risky because if a trade was to fail, then the trader could experience a catastrophe. However, with diversification, the risk is spread out so that regardless of what happens to some stocks, the trader still stands to be profitable.

At the core of diversification is the challenge posed by unsystematic risks. When some stocks or investments perform better than others, these risks are neutralized. Therefore, for a perfectly balanced portfolio, a trader should ensure that they only deal with non-correlated assets. This means that the assets respond in opposite ways or differently to market forces.

The ideal portfolio should contain between 25 and 30 different securities. This is the perfect way of ensuring that the risk levels are drastically reduced and the only expected outcomes are profitability.

In summary, diversification is a popular strategy that is used by both traders and investors. It makes use of a wide variety of securities in order to improve yield and mitigate against inherent and potential risks.

It is advisable to invest or trade in a variety of assets and not all from one class. For instance, a properly diversified portfolio should include assets such as currencies, options, stocks, bonds, and so on. This approach will increase the chances of profitability and minimize risks and exposure. Diversification is even better if assets are acquired across geographical regions as well.

Best Diversification Approach

Diversification focuses on asset allocation. It consists of a plan that endeavors to allocate funds or assets appropriately across a variety of investments. When an investor diversifies his or her portfolio, then there is some level of risk that has to be accepted. However, it is also advisable to devise an exit strategy so that the investor is able to let go of the asset and recoup their funds. This becomes necessary when a specific asset class is not yielding any worthwhile returns compared to others.

If an investor is able to create an aptly diversified portfolio, their investment will be adequately covered. An adequately diversified portfolio also allows room for growth. Appropriate asset allocation is highly recommended as it allows investors a chance to leverage risk and manage any possible portfolio volatility because different assets have varying reactions to adverse market conditions.

Investor Opinions on Diversifications

Different investors have varying opinions regarding the type of investment scenarios they consider being ideal. Numerous investors believe that a properly diversified portfolio will likely bring in a double-digit return despite prevailing market conditions. They also agree that in the worst-case situation there will be simply a general decrease in the value of the different assets. Yet with all this information out there, very few investors are actually able to achieve portfolio diversification.

So why are investors unable to simply diversify their portfolios appropriately? The answers are varied and diverse. The challenges encountered by investors in diversification include weighting imbalance, hidden correlation, underlying devaluation, and false returns, among others. While these challenges sound rather technical, they can easily be solved. The solution is also rather simple. By hacking these challenges, an investor will then be able to benefit from an aptly diversified platform.

The Process of Asset Class Allocation

There are different ways of allocating investments to assets. According to studies, most investors, including professional investors, portfolio managers, and seasoned traders rarely beat the indexes within their preferred asset class. It is also important to note that there is a visible correlation between the performance of an underlying asset class and the returns that an investor receives. In general, professional investors tend to perform more or less the same as an index within the same class asset.

Investment returns from a diversified portfolio can generally be expected to imitate the related asset class closely. Therefore, asset class choice is considered an extremely crucial aspect of an investment. In fact, it is the single most crucial aspect for the success of a particular asset class. Other factors, such as individual asset selection and market timing, only contribute about 6% of the variance in investment outcomes.

Wide Diversifications between Various Asset Classes

Diversification to numerous investors simply implies spreading their funds through a wide variety of stocks in different sectors such as health care, financial, energy, as well as medium caps, small, and large-cap companies. This is the opinion of your average investor. However, a closer look at this approach reveals that investors are simply putting their money in different sectors of stocks class. These asset classes can very easily fall and rise when the markets do.

A reliably diversified portfolio is one where the investor or even the manager is watchful and alert because of the hidden correlation that exists between different asset classes. This correlation can easily change with time, and there are several reasons for this. One reason is international markets. Many investors often choose to diversify their portfolios with international stocks.

However, there is also a noticeable correlation across the different global financial markets. This correlation is visible not just across European markets but also emerging markets from around the world. There is also a clear correlation between equities and fixed income markets, which are generally the hallmarks of diversification.

This correlation is actually a challenge and is probably a result of the relationship between structured financing and investment banking. Another factor that contributes to this correlation is the rapid growth and popularity of hedge funds. Take the case where a large international organization such as a hedge fund suffers losses in a particular asset class.

Should this happen, then the firm may have to dispose of some assets across the different asset classes. This will have a multiplier effect as numerous other investments, and other investors will, therefore, be affected even though they had diversified their portfolios appropriately. This is a challenge that affects numerous investors who are probably unaware of its existence. They are also probably unaware of how it should be rectified or avoided.

Realignment of Asset Classes

One of the best approaches to solving the correlation challenge is to focus on class realignment. Basically, asset allocation should not be considered as a static process. Asset class imbalance is a phenomenon that occurs when the securities markets develop, and different asset classes exhibit varied performance.

After a while, investors should assess their investments then diversify out of underperforming assets and instead shift this investment to other asset classes that are performing well and are profitable in the long term. Even then, it is advisable to be vigilant so that no one single asset class is over-weighted as other standard risks are still inherent. Also, a prolonged bullish market can result in overweighting one of the different asset classes which could be ready for a correction.

Diversification and the Relative Value

Investors sometimes find asset returns to be misleading, including veteran investors. As such, it is advisable to interpret asset returns in relation to the specific asset class performance. The interpretation should also take into consideration the risks that this asset class is exposed to and even the underlying currency.

When diversifying investments, it is important to think about diversifying into asset classes that come with different risk profiles. These should also be held in a variety of currencies. You should not expect to enjoy the same outcomes when investing in government bonds and technology stocks. However, it is recommended to endeavor to understand how each suits the larger investment objective.

Using such an approach, it will be possible to benefit more from a small gain from an asset within a market where the currency is increasing in value. This is as compared to a large gain from an asset within a market where the currency is in decline. As such, huge gains can translate into losses when the gains are reverted back to the stronger currency. This is the reason why it is advisable to ensure that proper research and evaluation of different asset classes are conducted.

Currencies Should Be Considered

Currency considerations are crucial when selecting asset classes to diversify in. Take the Swiss Franc for instance. It is one of the world's most stable currencies and has been that way since the 1940s. Because of this reason, this particular currency can be safely and reliably used to measure the performance of other currencies.

However, private investors sometimes take too long choosing and trading stocks. Such activities are both overwhelming and time-consuming. This is why, in such instances, it is advisable to approach this differently and focus more on the asset class. With this kind of approach, it is possible to be even more profitable. Proper asset allocation is crucial to successful investing. It enables investors to mitigate any investment risks as well as portfolio volatility. The reason is that different asset classes have different reactions to all the different market conditions.

Constructing a well thought out and aptly diversified portfolio, it is possible to have a stable and profitable portfolio that even outperforms the index of assets. Investors also have the opportunity to leverage against any potential risks because of different reactions by the different market.

83

Chapter 8: Momentum Trading

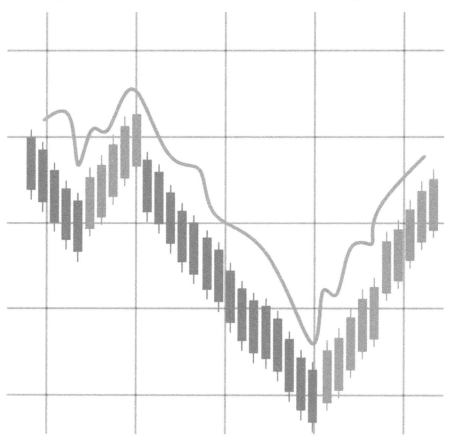

Momentum is at the heart of day trading as finding trades with the right amount of momentum is the only way you can reliably guarantee a profit on your trades. Luckily, it is not unrealistic to expect to find at least one underlying asset that is likely to move as much as 30 percent each day since all underlying assets with this much momentum all tend to share a few common technical indicators.

Momentum stock anatomy

While it might seem difficult to understand how anyone could expect to pick a stock with the right momentum out of the thousands of possible choices, the fact of the matter is that all high momentum stocks typically have several things in common. In fact, if you were given a list of 5,000 stocks, using the factors below you could likely come up with a list of 10 or less.

- Float: The first thing you are going to want to keep in mind is that the stocks with the highest momentum are generally going to have a float that is less than 100 million shares. Float refers to the total number of shares that are currently available and can be found by taking the total number of outstanding shares and subtracting out all those that are restricted or are, functionally speaking, no longer traded. Restricted shares are those that are currently in the midst of a lockup period or other, similar restriction. The less float a stock has, the more volatility it is going to contain. Stocks with smaller float tend to have low liquidity and a higher bid/ask spread.

- Daily charts: The next thing you are going to want to look for is stocks that are consistently beating their moving average and trending away from either the support or resistance depending on if you are following a positive or negative trend.

- Relative volume: You are also going to want to ensure that the stocks you are considering have a high amount of relative volume, with the minimum being twice what the current average is. The average you should consider in this case would be the current volume compared to the historical average for the stock in question. The standard volume is going to reset every night at midnight which means this is a great indicator when it comes to stocks that are seeing a higher-than-average amount of action right now.

- Catalyst: While not, strictly speaking, required, you may still find it helpful to look for stocks that are currently having their momentum boosted by external sources. This can include things like active investors, FDA announcements, and PR campaigns and earnings reports.

Exit indicators to watch

Besides knowing what a potentially profitable momentum trade looks like, you are also going to need to know what to look for to ensure that you can successfully get while the getting is good. Keep the following in mind and you will always be able to get out without having to sacrifice any of your hard-earned profits.

- Don't get greedy: It is important to set profit targets before you go into any trade, and then follow through on them when the trade turns in your favor. If you find yourself riding a stronger trend than you initially anticipated, the best choice is to instead sell off half of your holdings before setting a new and improved price target for the rest, allowing you to have your cake and eat it too.

- Red candles: If you are not quite at your price target and you come across a candle that closes in the red then this is a strong indicator that you should take what you have and exit ASAP. If you have already sold off half of your holdings at this point, however, then you are going to want to go ahead and hold through the first red candle as long as it doesn't go so far as to trigger your stop loss actively.

87

- Extension bar: An extension bar is a candle with a spike that causes dramatically increased profits. If this occurs, you want to lock in your profits as quickly as possible as it is unlikely to last very long. This is your lucky day, and it is essential to capitalize on it.

Choosing a screener

Another important aspect of using a momentum strategy correctly is using a quality stock screen in order to find stocks that are trending towards the extreme ends of the market based on the criteria outlined above. A good screener is a virtually indispensable tool when it comes to narrowing down the field of potential options on any given day, the best of the best even let you generate your own unique filters that display a list of stocks that meet a variety of different criteria. Below is a list of some of the most popular screeners on the market today.

- StockFetchter.com: StockFetcher.com is one of the more complicated screeners out there, but all that complexity comes with a degree of power that is difficult to beat. Its power comes from a virtually unlimited number of parameters that its users can add to filter, ensuring that you only see exactly the types of stocks you are looking for. It offers a free as well as a paid version, the free version allows you to see the top five stores that match your parameters while the paid version, $8.95 per month, shows you unlimited results.

- Finviz.com: This site offers a wide variety of different premade filters that are designed to return results on the most promising stocks for a given day. It is extremely user friendly as well and functions from three drop-down menus based on the type of indicator, technical, fundamental or descriptive, and lets you choose the criteria for each. The results can then be sorted in a myriad of different ways to make it as easy to find the types of stocks you are looking for as possible. The biggest downside to Finviz is that it uses delayed data which means it is going to be most effective for those who run evening screens, so they are ready to go when the market opens.

- Chartmill.com: This site allows users to filter stocks based on a number of predetermined criteria including things like price, performance, volume, technical indicators and candlestick patterns. It also offers up a number of more specialized indicators including things like squeeze plays, intensity, trend and pocket pivots. This site works based on a credit system, and every user is given 6,000 credits each month for free. Every scan costs a few hundred credits so you should be able to take advantage of a variety of their tools virtually free of charge. Additional credits then cost $10 per 10,000 or an unlimited option available for about $30 per month.

- Stockrover.com: This tool is specifically designed to cater to the Canadian market in addition to the US stock market. It offers up a variety of fundamental filters in addition to technical and performance-based options. This tool also allows you to track stocks that are near their established lows and high, those that may be gaining momentum and even those that are seeing a lot of love from various hedge funds. Users also can create custom screens as well as unique equations for even more advanced screening. Users can also backtest their ideas to make sure that everything is working as intended. While their basic options are free to use, the more complicated choices are gated behind a paywall that costs $250 for a year's subscription.

Know your filters

Day trading is about more than finding stocks that are high in volume, it is also about finding those that are currently experiencing a higher-than-average degree of movement as well. The following filters will help ensure that the stocks you find have plenty of both.

- Steady volatility: In order to trade stocks that are extremely volatile with as little research as possible, the following criterion is an excellent place to start. It is important to use a minimum of 50 days, though 75 or 100 will produce even more reliable results overall. Results of this magnitude will show that the stock in question has moved a significant amount over the past few months which means it is likely to continue to do so for the near future. The second criterion will determine the amount you should be willing to pay per share and can be altered based on your personal preferences.

  The third criterion will determine the level of volume that you find acceptable for the given timeframe. The example will look for volume that is greater than four million shares within the past month. From there, it will eliminate leverage ETFs from the results which can be eliminated if you are interested in trading ETFs. Finally, the add column will show the list of stocks with the largest amount of volume and the greatest overall amount of movement. Selecting these columns will then rank the results from least to greatest based on the criteria provided.

- Monitor regularly: Alternately, you may want to do a daily search to determine the stocks that will experience the greatest range of movement in the coming hours. To do so, you will want to create a new list of stocks every evening to ensure that you will be ready to go when the market opens. This list can then be made up of stocks that have shown higher volatility in the former day either in terms of gains or in terms of losses. Adding in volume to these criteria will then help to make sure the results will likely continue to generate the kind of volume that day trading successfully requires. Useful filters for this search include an average volume that is greater than one million and the more you increase the minimum volume the fewer results you'll see.

When using this strategy, it is especially important to pick out any stocks that are likely to see major news releases before the following day as these are almost guaranteed to make the price move in a number of random directions before ultimately settling down. As such, it is often best to wait until after the details of the release are known and you can more accurately determine what the response is, though not so long that you miss out on the combination of high volume and high volatility. If you don't already have an earnings calendar bookmarked, the one available for free from Yahoo! Finance is well respected.

- Monitor intraday volatility: Another option that is worth considering is doing your researching during the day as a means of determining which stocks are experiencing the greatest overall amount of movement at the moment. A vast majority of trading platforms provide this information in real-time, so it is easy to keep up to date on the changes that are happening at the moment. For example, if a stock opens at a point down 10 percent from its former close and stays there you can then assume that there is no one biting on the action that the stock has available.

Chapter 9: Top Day Trading Tools

The main tools you'll need for day trading are an online broker and an order execution platform. It goes without saying that you'll also need a very good internet connection and a computer on which to execute your trades on the platform. And if you're not part of a day trading community yet, you'll also need a stock scanner.

The Broker

You'll need a very good broker, who'll be your access to the securities market you plan to day trade in, e.g., the stock market. Take note that your broker can't just be good: it must be very good. Why?

Since you can't access the stock market or other securities markets directly, you'll need to go through a broker. Even if you choose your SIPs correctly, you can still lose money in your trades if your broker's slow to execute your order at your target price or if their system suffers from frequent glitches.

It can be challenging to choose a broker because there are many of them out there. Some offer top service but are expensive while some charge very low fees, but their service is not good.

Minimum Equity Requirement

The United States Securities and Exchange Commission (SEC) and the Financial Industry Regulatory Authority (FINRA) enforce rules on people who day trade. They use the term Pattern Day Trader to qualify those who can engage in day trading with stock brokerage firms operating in the United States.

They qualify pattern day traders as those who day trades, i.e., takes and closes positions within the same day, at least four times in the last five business days. The SEC and FINRA require that pattern day traders must have a minimum equity balance of $25,000 in their brokerage account before they day trade. When the equity balance falls below this amount for one reason or another, brokers are compelled to prohibit pattern day traders from executing new day trades until they're able to bring their equity back up to at least $25,000.

Many newbie day traders, especially those who only have this minimum amount, look at this rule as more of a hindrance to day trading glory rather than a protective fence against day trading tragedies. They don't realize that it's meant to keep them from taking excessive day trading risks that can easily wipe out their trading capitals in a jiffy because of their brokers' commissions and fees.

While this rule is the minimum requirement under the law, many brokers and dealers may use a stricter definition of a pattern day trader for purposes of transacting with them. The best thing to do is to clarify this minimum equity requirement with your chosen broker to avoid confusion later.

If you can't afford the $25,000 minimum equity requirement for day trading, you can opt to trade with an offshore broker instead. They're brokerage firms that operate outside the United States, such as Capital Markets Elite Group Limited, which operates out of Trinidad and Tobago. Because these brokers operate outside the jurisdiction of FINRA, they're not subject to the pattern day trader rule. This means you're also not subject to the same minimum amount.

But before you think of trading with offshore brokers, keep in mind that these brokers are beyond the juridical reach of the SEC and FINRA. This means if anything goes wrong, you can't count on the Federal Government to help you out. If you really want to use them to avoid the pattern day trader rule, just make sure to limit the amount of day trading equity you'll place with such brokers to an amount that you're comfortable risking or losing.

Direct-Access and Conventional Brokers

Conventional brokers normally reroute their customer's orders, including yours, to other firms through some sort of pre-agreed upon order processing scheme. Thus, executing your orders through conventional brokers involve more steps and can take significantly more time. And when it comes to day trading, speed is essential.

Conventional brokers are often referred to as full-service brokers because they tend to provide customers with other services such as market research and investment advice, among others. Because of these "extras," their commissions and fees are usually much higher than direct-access brokers. Conventional or full-service brokers are ideal for long-term investors and swing traders because they're not as particular with the speed of trade executions as day traders are.

Compared to full-service or conventional brokers, direct-access brokers focus more on the speed of trade executions than research and advisory services. And because they often skip the extra services to focus on providing fast and easy access to the stock market, they charge less commissions and fees. This has earned many of them the alias "discount brokers."

Direct-access brokers use very powerful computer programs and provide customers online platforms through which they can directly trade the stock market, whether it's the NASDAQ or the NYSE. And while they provide the necessary trade execution speeds required in day trading, they're not perfect and they have their share of challenges.

Real-Time Market Data

Unlike long-term investors and swing traders who only need end-of-day price data that are available for free online, day traders need real-time data as the trading day unfolds because they need to get in and out of positions within a matter of hours, minutes, or even seconds. And unfortunately, access to real-time intraday price data isn't free and you'll need to pay monthly fees to your direct-access broker or the platform owner (if different from the brokerage firm) for them. Just ask your direct-access broker for details on their monthly fees for access to real-time day trading data.

Two of the most basic types of data that you'll need to look at as a day trader are the bid and ask prices. The bid prices are the prices at which other traders and investors are willing to buy a stock. The ask prices are the prices at which other traders and investors are willing to sell a stock.

The bid and ask prices are arranged such that the best price is at the top. The best ask price, on the other hand, is the lowest price at which sellers are willing to sell. It's considered the best price from the perspective of buyers. Bid and ask prices also indicate the number of shares that other traders and investors are willing to buy or sell them at specific prices.

The bid prices are usually listed on the left side while the ask prices are usually listed on the right such that the best bid and ask prices are right beside each other. If you want to execute your buy orders immediately, you "buy up" the best ask price. If you want to immediately execute your sell orders, "sell down" at the best bid price.

The Day Trading Orders

The three most important types of day trading orders are market, limit, and marketable limit orders.

Market orders refer to orders to buy or sell stocks at their current market prices for immediate execution. If you remember from earlier, these refer to buying up at the best current ask price or selling down at the best bid price.

Depending on market conditions and subsequent price movements during the day, market orders may be the worst or best prices to trade in. For example: if you send a market order to sell when the bid-ask prices are $1.00-$1.05 and the by the time your order hits the market, the bid-ask prices shift to $0.95-$1.01, your sell order will be done at $0.95. In this example, your sell proceeds get cut by a minimum of five cents multiplied by the number of shares you sold.

On the other hand, let's say you sent a buy market order when the current bid-ask prices are $1.10-$1.15. If the bid-ask prices change to

$1.12-$1.17 by the time your market order reaches the market, you'll end up paying $0.02 cents more for every share of that stock.

Only market makers and professional traders with a lot of day trading expertise and experience can benefit from market orders. For retail day traders like you and I, we should avoid market orders as much as possible.

Hardware

You must avoid using wireless or Bluetooth keyboards and mice for day trading. Why? Here are some things that can happen with wireless keyboards and mice that can negatively impact your day trading activities:

They put you at risk of getting low on power or getting completely drained at the height of your day trading activities, which will immobilize you from day trading until you're able to switch to another keyboard and put you at risk of missing out on key prices.

They can erroneously execute keystrokes multiple times, particularly when low in power; and they can fail to send orders if the signal's interrupted by low power or other signal interruptions.

101

Aside from sticking to wired keyboards and mice for your trading, make sure you have a set of backups in case something happens, like spilling drinks on them. Better safe than sorry.

Stock Pick Scanners and Watch lists

Because there are thousands of stocks that are eligible for day trading every single trading day, it's impossible to manually scan the market for SIPs fast enough to make timely day trades. That's why you'll need to use a market-scanning software to shortlist your day trading choices. One of the most popular market-scanning software in the market today that you can consider for your day trading activities is Trade Ideas at **www.tradeideas.com**.

Day Trading Community

No man (or woman, to be more gender-sensitive) is an island, as the saying goes. This includes day traders.

Day trading can be overwhelming for newbies and one of the best ways that you can more easily navigate through it is by joining a community of day traders. There, you can find technical, intellectual, and dare I say even emotional support as you begin traversing the road less traveled called day trading. You can glean useful pieces of day trading information such as which stocks are about to be in day trading play and new day trading methods and tactics, among others.

Get Your Education

You need to make sure you are educated on your topic. You want to treat day trading as your new career. Therefore, you should make sure that you have researched your topic and consider yourself an expert on day trading. Of course, there are lessons that you are going to learn naturally as you start day trading. Experienced traders believe that people should take about three to four months and practice with simulators before practicing with money.

Build Your Business Plan

You need to have a business plan. One of the biggest factors to remember when you are getting into day trading is you must treat it like any other serious career choice. With any business you would start up and get into, you will have a business plan. You need to make sure your education is part of your business plan (for example, any classes you are planning on taking). You also must make sure your schedule, the tools you will use, platforms, technology, software, and anything else incorporated in your business is a part of your business plan.

Another thing to remember when creating your business plan is to look at every single detail. You do not want to miss something or think it is fine to skip over anything. On top of this, you want to make sure that you look at your business plan often, even after you start trading. In fact, it is best if you look at your business plan at least once a month, if not more.

Chapter 10: Options Day Trading Rules for Success

To develop into the options day trader you want to be, being disciplined is necessary. There are options day trading rules that can help you develop that necessary discipline.

Knowing common mistakes helps you avoid many of these mistakes and takes away much of the guesswork. Having rules to abide by helps you avoid these mistakes as well.

Rule #1 Be Mentally, Physically, and Emotionally Prepared Every Day

This is a mentally, physically, and emotionally tasking career, and you need to be able to meet the demands of this career. That means keeping your body, mind, and heart in good health at all times. Ensure that you schedule a time for self-care every day. That can be as simple as taking the time to read for recreation to having an elaborate self-care routine carved out in the evenings.

Not keeping your mind, heart, and head in optimum health means that they are more likely to fail you. Signs that you need to buckle up and care for yourself more diligently include being constantly tired, being short-tempered, feeling preoccupied, and being easily distracted.

To ensure you perform your best every day, here a few tasks that you need to perform:

• Get the recommended amount of sleep daily. This is between 7 and 9 hours for an adult.

• Practice a balanced diet. The brain and body need adequate nutrition to work their best. Include fruits, complex carbs, and veggies in this diet and reduce the consumption of processed foods.

• Eat breakfast, lunch, and dinner every day. Fuel your mind and body with the main meals. Eating a healthy breakfast is especially important because it helps set the tone for the rest of the day.

• Exercise regularly. Being inactive increases your risk of developing chronic diseases like heart disease, certain cancers, and terrible health consequences. Exercise reduces those risks and allows your brain to function better, which is a huge advantage for an options day trader.

Rule #2 Know Your Limits

You may be tempted to trade as much as possible to develop a winning monthly average, but that strategy will have the opposite effect and land you with a losing average. Remember that every option trader needs careful consideration before a contract is set up. Never overtrade and tie up your investment fund.

Rule #3 Start Small to Grow a Big Portfolio

Remember that you are still learning options trading and developing an understanding of the financial market. Do not jump the gun even if you are eager. After you have practiced paper trading, start with smaller options positions, and steadily grow your standing as you get a lay of the options day trading land. This strategy allows you to keep your losses to a minimum and develop a systematic way of entering positions.

Rule #4 Have a Realistic Expectation

It is sad to say that many people who enter the options trading industry are doing so to make quick money. Options trading is not a get-rich-quick scheme. It is a distinguished career that has made many people rich, but that is only because these people have put in the time, effort, study, and dedication to learning the craft and mastering it. Mastery does not happen overnight, and beginner options day traders need to be prepared for that learning curve and have the courage to stick with day trading options even when it becomes tough.

Losses are also part of the game. No trading style or strategy will guarantee gains all the time. The best options traders have a winning percentage of about 80% and a losing average of approximately 20%. That is why an options day trader needs to be a good money manager and a good risk manager. Be prepared for eventual losses and be prepared to minimize those losses.

Rule #5 Do Your Homework Daily

You need to get knowledge so that you have the basis for making decisions. When you know all there is to know about options, you know what to buy and when to sell, and learn which ones to watch. You are then more comfortable making the right decisions. Always evaluate your choices and see what you have gained or lost so far for taking some steps. Understanding the mistakes you made guides you to make better decisions in the future.

Rule #6 Analyze Your Daily Performance

To determine if the options day trading style and strategies that you have adopted are working for you, you need to track your performance. At the most basic, this needs to be done because you are trading options daily. It allows you to notice patterns in your profit and loss. This can lead to you determining the why and how of these gains and losses. These determinations lead to fine-tuning your daily processes for maximum returns.

Rule #7 Do Not Be Greedy

This refers to a selfish desire to get more money than you need from a trade. When the desire to get more than you can usually make takes over your decision-making process, you are looking at failure.

Greed is seen to be more detrimental than fear. It places you in a situation where you spend your capital faster than you return it. It pushes you to act when you should not be acting at all.

When you are greedy, you end up acting irrationally. Irrational trading behavior can be overtrading, overleveraging, holding onto trades for too long, or chasing different markets. The more greed you have, the more foolish you act. If you reach a point at which greed takes over from common sense, you are overdoing it.

Rule #8 Pay Attention to Volatility

Volatility speaks to how likely a price change will occur over a specific amount of time on the financial market. Volatility can work for an options day trader or against the options day trader. It all depends on what the options day trader is trying to accomplish and his or her current position.

Many external factors affect volatility, and such factors include the economic climate, global events, and news reports. Strangles and straddles strategies are great for use in volatile markets.

There are different types of volatility, and they include:

• Price volatility, which describes how the price of an asset increases or decreases based on the supply and demand of that asset.

• Historical volatility, which is a measure of how an asset has performed over the last 12 months.

• Implied volatility, which is a measure of how an asset will perform in the future.

Rule #9 Use the Greeks

Option traders use the Greeks to measure risk in their option positions and their combined positions or portfolios. Greeks are extremely important, and it should be the goal of anyone wanting to trade or invest in options to gain an intuitive understanding. An intuitive understanding of the Greeks will provide you with an understanding of the risk in your option position(s) and greatly contribute to your success as an options trader.

111

Delta

The Delta represents the amount the value of the option should change with a $1 move (up or down) in the Underlying stock price. Delta means change.

Vega

Vega measures the impact of a 1.00% change in volatility on the theoretical value of an option. It is important to monitor Vega to properly understand the risk in both your long and short positions.

Theta

Theta measures the general daily decay of the option premium, assuming no changes in the stock price and volatility. The life of an option is finite with a defined expiration and, therefore, every day, it decays in value—Theta measures this decay.

Gamma

Gamma simply represents the Delta's change for a given change in the underlying stock—it is the "Delta of the Delta."

Gamma shows the potential for your option position to "move" in terms of value. Note that Gamma can be either positive or negative.

Positive Gamma is generally good for your position, and negative Gamma is generally bad for your position.

Rho

Rho is a measure of the options pricing's sensitivity to a change in the risk-free interest rate. Since interest rates don't change by that much or that often these days, Rho isn't paid much attention to.

Rule #10 Be flexible

Many options day traders find it difficult to try trading styles and strategies they are unfamiliar with. While the saying, "Do not fix it if it is not broken," is quite true, you will never become more effective and efficient in this career if you do not step out of your comfort zone at least once in a while. Stick with what works but allow room for the consideration that there may be better alternatives.

Chapter 11: Psychology Discipline

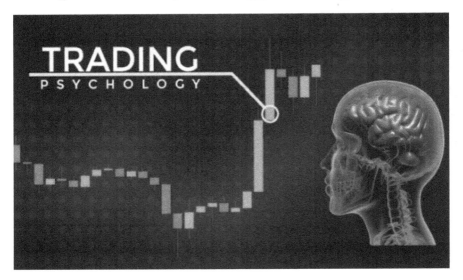

Trading with Emotions

It is common for traders to have their emotions and feelings jumbled up when day trading, from the highs and the lows they experience from the market. This is a far outcry from the confident self that a trader usually poses before the markets open, bubbling up with excitement over the money and profits that they intend to make. Emotions in trading can mess up and impair your judgment and your ability to make wise decisions. Day trading is not to be carried out without emotions, but rather as a trader, you should know how to work your way around them, making them work for your good. A clear levelheaded and stable mind should be kept at all times, whether your profits are on the rise or whether you are on a losing streak. This is not to mean that as a trader, you are to disconnect from your emotions.

Greed

A trader may be fueled to earn more money by checking their balances in their accounts and seeing it be of a low level. While this may be a motivator to work hard, some traders take it too far, wanting to earn a lot of money right there and then. They make mistakes while trading that has reverse effects than the intended ones.

Taking Unnecessary Risks

Greed for more money will seek to convince the trader to take risks that are not worth it so as to achieve a certain financial threshold in the trading account. This risk-taking will most likely end up in losses. The risky traders may take risks such as high leverage that they hope will work in their favor, but at the same time may have them making huge losses.

Making an Overtrade

Due to the urge to make more and more money, a trader may extend over long periods of time trading. Commonly these efforts are in vain, for overtrading through the highs and the lows of the market put a trader in a position where their accounts can be wiped off as a result of greed. Not putting into account, the time of trading and plunging into opening up trades without having done an analysis will most likely result in a loss.

Improper Profit and Loss Comprehension

Wanting to earn a lot of money within a short period of time will have a trader not closing a trade that is losing, maintaining the losses, and on the other hand, over riding on profit-making trade until a reverse in the market happens, canceling out all the gains made.

Fear

Fear can work in both directions, as a limit to an over-trade or also as a limit to making profits. A trader may close a trade so as to avert a loss, the action motivated by fear. A trader may also close a trade too early, even when on a winning streak in making gains, in fear that the market will reverse and that there will be losses. In both scenarios, fear is the motivator, working in avoiding failure and success at the same time.

The Fear to Fail

The fear of failing in trading may inhibit a trader from opening up trades and just watch as the market changes and goes in cycles when doing nothing. The fear of failing in trading is an inhibitor to success. It prevents a trader from executing what could have been a successful trade.

The Fear to Succeed

This type of fear in trading psychology will make a trader lose out his profits to the market when there was an opportunity to do otherwise. It works in a self-harming way in the market scenarios. Such traders in this category fear having too much profit and allow losses to run, all while aware of their activities and the losses they are going to make.

Bias in Trading

There are several market biases that a trader may tend to make that may be a result of an emotional play, which traders are advised against. In the psychology of trading, these biases may influence a trader to make unwise and uncalculated trading decisions that may

117

prove to be loss-making ones. Even when the trading biases are in focus, as a trader, you have to be aware of the emotions in you and come up with ways to keep them in check and maintain a cool head in your trading window.

Bias in Overconfidence

It is a common occurrence with traders, especially new traders, that when you make a trade with huge profits, you get euphoric in the state of winning. You want to go on opening up trades with the belief that your analysis cannot go wrong, boiling down to the profits and gains you've made.

This should not be the case. One cannot be too overexcited and overconfident in the analysis skills that you believe you cannot make a loss. The market is a volatile one, and therefore the cards can change at any given time, and when they do, the over-excited and overconfident trader becomes a disappointed one.

Bias in Confirming Trades

In trading psychology, the bias in confirmation of a trade you have already made, justifying it, is one of the factors that waste a lot of time and money for traders. This type of bias is mostly associated with professional traders. After making a trade, they go back to evaluate and analyze the trade they just made, trying to prove that it was the correct one, whether they sailed according to the market. They waste a lot of time digging for information that they are already aware of. They could also be proving that the mistake they made in opening a wrong trade and making a wrong move was a correct one.

Bias in Anchoring on Obsolete Strategies

This type of bias in the psychology of trading applies to the traders that rely so much on outdated information and obsolete strategies that do more harm than good to their trading success.

Anchoring on the correct but irrelevant information when trading might make the trader susceptible to making losses, a blow to the traders who are always lazy to dig up for new information on the market. Keeping up with the current events and factors that may have an impact on the market is one of the key aspects of having a successful trading career.

Bias in Avoiding Losses

Trading with the motive to avert losses usually boils down to the fear factor. There are some traders whose trading patterns and their trading windows are controlled by fear of making losses. Having gains and making profits is not a motivation to them when fear hinders them from opening trades that could have otherwise been profitable. They also close trades too early, even when making profits in a bid to avert imaginary losses.

Psychology Affecting Traders' Habits

Psychological aspects affect habits in trading, the mistakes, and the winning strategies that a trader comes up with. Explained below are the negative habits that many traders make with the influence of psychology on their habits.

Trading Without a Strategy

With no trading strategy and plan, a trader will face challenges with no place to refer to the anticipated end result. A proper strategy should be drawn by a trader to be a referencing point when facing a problem in trading in the market. It should be a clearly constructed plan, detailing what to do in certain situations and which type of trading patterns to employ in different case scenarios. Trading without a strategy is akin to trading to lose your money.

Lack of Money Management Plans

Money management plans are one of the main aspects of trading, and without solid strategies in this, it is difficult to make progress in making gains in the trades opened. As a trader, you have to abide by certain principles that will guide you in how to spend the money in your account in opening up trades and ensuring that profits ensue from that.

Wanting to Be Always Right

Some traders always go against the market, placing their desire of what manner they would like the market to behave in. They do not follow the sign that the market points to, but rather they follow their own philosophy, not doing proper analysis and always wanting to be right.

Remedying the Effects of Psychological Habits

Coming Up with Clear Cut Goals

Drawing clear and concise goals and strategies to trade helps a trader in having a vision of trading and not just doing it for the sake of trading. Writing down goals also works to improve the confidence levels of the trader. Working with a well comprehensive strategy is a profit-making plan in the market.

Setting Up Rules for Trading

Rules for the trader work for the good in ensuring discipline in trading. As a trader, you should come up with rules that govern the time of the day that you start trading, the time that you close your trades, and whether or not you trade on a daily basis, or whatever your trading window is. Rules are the backbone of successful trading; when to close a losing trade and at the same time when to close a winning one.

Initializing Money Management Strategies

Coming up with money strategies is not enough, but also actualizing the strategies is equally important.

Money management strategies are of great importance in ensuring that a trader's profitability is put first, putting into consideration the risk of loss. Put the money strategy into action to avoid trading haphazardly and trading with emotions.

Chapter 12: Dos and Don'ts of Day Trading

Dos of Day Trading

Risk capital

You have to understand that the stock market is a very volatile place, and anything can happen within a matter of a few seconds. You have to be prepared for anything that it throws at you. In order to prepare for it, you have to make use of risk capital. Risk capital refers to money that you are willing to risk. You have to convince yourself that even if you lose the money that you have invested then it will not be a big deal for you. For that, you have to make use of your own money and not borrow from anyone, as you will start feeling guilty about investing it. Decide on a set number and invest it.

Research

You have to conduct thorough research on the market before investing in it. Don't think you will learn as you go. That is only possible if you at least know the basics. You have to remain interested in gathering information that is crucial for your investments and it will only come about if you put in some hard work towards it. Nobody is asking you to stay up and go through thick textbooks. All you have to do is go through books and websites and gather enough information to help you get started on the right foot.

Diversification

You have to stress on diversification in your portfolio. You don't want all the money to go into the same place. Think of it as a way to increase your stock's potential. You have to choose different sectors and diverse stocks to invest in. you should also choose one of the different types of investments as they all contribute towards attaining

124

a different result. Diversification is mostly seen as a tool to cut down on risk and it is best that you not invest any more than 5% in any one of the securities.

Stop loss

You have to understand the importance of a stop-loss mechanism. A stop-loss technique is used to safeguard your capital. Now say for example you invest $100 and buy shares priced at $5 each. You have to place a stop loss at around $4 in order to stop it from going down any further. Now you will wonder as to why you have to place the stop loss and undergo one, well, by doing so, you will actually be saving your money to a large extent. You won't have to worry about the value slipping further down and can carry on with your trade.

Take a loss

It is fine to take a loss from time to time. Don't think of it as a big hurdle. You will have the chance the convert the loss into a profit. You have to remain confident and invested. You can take a loss on a bad investment that is not going your way. You can also take a loss on an investment that you think is a long hold and will not work for you in the short term. Taking a few losses is the only way in which you can learn to trade well in the market.

These form the different dos of the stock market that will help you with your intraday trades.

Don'ts of Day Trading

No planning

Do not make the mistake of going about investing in the market without a plan in tow. You have to plan out the different things that you will do in the market and go about it the right way. This plan should include how much you will invest in the market, where you will invest, how you will go about it etc. No planning will translate to getting lost in the stock market, which is not a good sign for any investor.

Over relying on a broker

You must never over-rely on a broker. You have to make your own decisions and know what to do and when. The broker will not know whether an investment is good for you. He will only be bothered about his profits. If he is suggesting something, then you should do your own research before investing in the stock. The same extends to emails that you might receive through certain sources. These emails are spams and meant to dupe you. So, don't make the mistake of trusting everything that you read.

Message boards

You have to not care about message boards. These will be available on the Internet and are mostly meant to help people gather information. But there will be pumpers and bashers present there. Pumpers will force people to buy a stock just to increase their value and bashers will force people to sell all their stocks just because they want the value to go down. Both types of people are dangerous, as they will abandon the investors just as soon as their motive is fulfilled. So, you have to be quite careful with it.

Wrong calculations

Some people make the mistake of calculating wrong. They will not be adept at math and will end up with wrong figures. This is a potential danger to all those looking to increase their wealth potential. If you are not good at calculating, then download an app that will do it for you or carry a calculator around to do the correct calculations.

The motive is to make the right calculations and increase your wealth potential.

Copy strategies

Do not make the mistake of copying someone else's strategies. You have to come up with something that is your own and not borrowed from someone else. If you end up borrowing, then you will not be able to attain the desired results. You have to sit with your broker and come up with a custom strategy that you can employ and win big.

These form the different don'ts of the stock market that will help you keep troubles at bay.

Chapter 13: Trading Psychology

If every Tom, Dick, and Harry could be a day trader, then the career would be oversaturated. The fact is that becoming a day trader is not for everyone (becoming a successful one, that is). To find success as a day trader, you need to be oriented in a certain way mentally to get the job done right. Let's talk about the psychological traits a trader needs to have to be profitable.

There's a lot of things to consider when day trading, and I've created a magazine that covers a few of them. I cover some super important stuff like how to **pick profitable stocks** to **trading strategy.** This is my magazine I was talking about earlier in the book.

Successful Day Trading Psychology

Even if you know and understand all the essential skills to be a day trader, it all amounts to nothing if you do not have a day trader's mindset. It would be like entering a car race with a bicycle and expecting to cross the finish line first. Getting your mental wavelength aligned with a day trader's is extremely important. That wavelength consists of thinking quickly on your feet, being self-disciplined, and controlling your emotions.

Let's start by talking about the importance of managing your emotions first. Excitement and anticipation can go a long way in fueling your drive on this day trading highway. It's when day traders are motivated by greed or fear that the wheels start coming loose.

On the next point of developing an effectual mindset for day trading—which is being able to roll with the punches and make quick decisions—there needs to be a balance. Of course, there are times when you need to enter and exit trades at the snap of a finger. That requires you to have the presence of mind to weigh the pros and cons of those trades. The point that negatively tips the scales is when day traders make snap decisions that are not backed by logic or experience but by emotions. You have to control your emotions when you make trades, or sooner or later, you will get the short end of the stick. Many day traders, even experienced ones, sometimes deal with fear. Their fear may stem from losing out on a trade or other factors, but the fear always means that the day trader reacts to something that threatens their position. That threat is typically directed at the potential profit that he or she will earn. Effective risk management is the only way to get past this natural emotional response. Most of the time, the fear that we feel in any aspect of life is overblown. Effective risk management helps you see the true magnitude of the things that you fear.

Greed is a troubling condition when it comes to day trading. "Pigs get slaughtered." That is a Wall Street saying that addresses the scenario of traders and investors trying to play out positions for too long to gain more. This tactic usually backfires.

The truth is that many people get into day trading to make a quick buck. Or, they believe that day trading is an enchanted pathway to great wealth. Of course, there is occasionally the case of someone hitting gold right out of the gate with day trading, but that is not the norm. Therefore, being greedy and making trades based on disillusion will only lead to catastrophe. Greed is a natural inclination to get more, and it is difficult to overcome in most cases. Still, it can be done with rational thinking and working based on an effective trading plan.

Controlling your emotions and making decisions that work for you instead of against you all comes down to self-discipline. You can only be a great day trader if you set a path for yourself and stay on it despite the obstacles. Things are not always going to go your way (welcome to this thing called life), and you have to know how to remain firm instead of being swayed by the current swing of things. A great way to be more self-disciplined in your day trading is by setting up rules for yourself about operating your trading business. That leads me to discuss our next day trading essential, which is creating a day trading plan.

Connect with other day traders in our community for support and knowledge. We learn faster when we all collaborate and connect. It would be great to have you.

Psychological and Technical Aspects of Determining Which Stock to Buy

Developing a trading plan is the first thing you need to do when you commit to this career. This will list your motivation for starting and sticking with this field. You also should look at the resources available to you. Plan how you'll build on your resources, define your daily trading approach, set goals, and so much more. Having no trading plan is a common sign that greed is a day trader's motivation because it shows that the trader did not sit down to do his or her homework.

Having a trading plan ensures that you do not act on your emotions while you are day trading. As part of ensuring that you make the maximum profit possible, have a road map guiding you. Your trading plan serves as your guide.

Therefore, before you start trading, or even paper trading (which means practicing without real money), you need to sit down and determine:

- What your long-term and short-term goals are

- How much money you will be able to invest in day trading

133

- How much time you will be able to commit to day trading and whether it will be every day

- What type of securities you would like to trade

- What strategies you will use to find opportunities in the stock market

- How much you are willing to risk with every trade, and what determines that risk

- Your rules for risk management

- What strategy you will use to ensure that losses are minimal

- What strategies you will use to figure out which stocks and other securities are worthy of your investment

These are only a few of the determinations that need to be made when creating a trading plan. A lot goes into creating an effective trading plan, which is typically not done in one sitting. Just like creating a business plan, you need to keep your emotions out of the process and allow your logical brain to guide you. Once you have formularized this plan and it is sound, this is a tool that will enable

134

you to grow and progress in the long-term and the short-term. One of the best things about an effective trading plan is that it summarizes your psychology. Let's face it, there are times when we all slip up. The brain is a fickle thing, prone to changing directions in thought quickly. Brains. Can't live with them, can't live without them, am I right? Luckily, having a trading plan allows you to rely on rationality and reasoning rather than your mind's whims.

The trading plan also allows you to notice what works for you as a day trader and what does not. It sets up the precedent for you to notice trends in your actions and build on the most profitable actions for you. Your trading plan is fluid and can be changed at any time. I highly encourage you to set up a schedule for regularly updating your trading plan weekly or monthly to incorporate new ideas and eliminate bad ones. That will help you stay on course with what you have envisioned for yourself and your trading career.

The last thing I would like to mention when creating a trading plan is this: do not limit yourself. Allow yourself to dream big. Realize that the sky's the limit with trading, even though it takes work to build the career you desire. The power of dreaming big is that flooding your brain with images of you succeeding allows you to be better positioned to manifest those visions. Do not limit yourself to thinking that you can make just a few hundred dollars a month by day trading. Many day traders make hundreds of thousands and millions of dollars every year day trading. Nothing is stopping you from accomplishing the same thing except you and your psychological approach to this career.

Chapter 14: Risk Management Techniques

When people think of day trading, they only think of potential profits, not losses. Therefore, day trading attracts so many people, they don't see the risk of losses. In stock markets, various events can trigger losses for investors and traders, which are beyond their control. These events can be economic conditions such as recession, geopolitical changes, changes in the central bank policies, natural disasters, or sometimes terror attacks.

This is the market risk; the potential of losing money due to unknown and sudden factors. These factors affect the overall performance of stock markets, and regardless of how careful one is while day trading, the possibility of market risk is always present, which can cause losses.

137

The market risk is known as the systematic risk because it influences the entire stock market. There is also a nonsystematic risk, which affects only a specific industry or company. Long-term investors tackle this risk by diversification in their investment portfolio.

Unlike investors, day traders have no method to neutralize market risk, but they can avoid it by keeping track of financial and business events, news, and economic calendars. For example, stock markets are very sensitive to the central banks' rate policies and become highly volatile on those days. Nobody knows what kind of policy any central bank will adopt in its monetary meeting. But day traders can check the economic calendar and know which day these meetings will take place. They can avoid trading on those days and reduce the risk of loss in trading.

Therefore, knowledge of stock markets and being aware of what is happening in the financial world is essential for day traders. Many successful traders have a policy of staying away from trading on days when any major economic event will take place, or a major decision will be announced. For example, on the day when the result of an important election is declared; any big company's court case decision comes in, or a central banks' policy meeting takes place. On such days, speculative trading dominates stock markets and market risk is very high. Similarly, on a day when any company announces earnings results, its stock price fluctuates wildly, increasing the market risk in trading of that stock.

In day trading, there is always a risk that you will lose money. Now, if you want to start day trading as a career, you need to learn a few techniques that will reduce and manage the risk of potential losses. By taking steps to manage the risk, you reduce the potential day trading losses.

To stay in the day trading business for the long term, you must protect your trading capital. By reducing the risk of losses, you open the possibilities of future profits and a sustainable day trading business.

If you plan well, prepare your trading strategies before starting to trade; you increase the possibility of a stable trading practice which can lead to profits. Therefore, it is essential to prepare your trading plans every day, create trading strategies and follow your trading rules. These three things can make or break your day trading business. Professional day traders always plan their trades first and then trade their plans. This can be understood by an example of two imaginary traders. Suppose there are two traders, trading in the same stock market, trading the same stock. One of them has prepared his trading plan and knows when and how he will trade. The other trader has done no planning and is just sitting there, taking the on-the-spot decisions for buying or selling the stock. Who do you think will be more successful? The one who is well prepared, or the one who has no inkling of what he will do the next second?

The second risk management technique is using stop orders. Use these orders to decide to fix your stop -loss and profit booking points, which will take emotions out of your decision-making process, and automatically cut the losses or book the profit for you.

Many a time, profitable trade turns into loss-making because markets change their trend, but traders do not exit their positions, hoping to increase profits. Therefore, it is necessary to keep a profit booking point and exit the profitable trades at that point. Keeping a fix profit booking point can also help you calculate your returns with every trade and help you avoid taking the unnecessary risk for further trades.

Taking emotions out of day trading is a very important requirement for profitable trading. Do not prejudge the trend in stock markets, which many day traders do and trade against markets, ending with losses.

Using Risk-Reward Ratio

Day trading is done for financial rewards and the good thing is, you can always calculate how much risk you take on every trade and how much reward you can expect. The risk-reward ratio represents the expected reward and expected risk traders can earn on the investment of every dollar.

The risk-reward ratio can excellently indicate your potential profits and potential loss, which can help you in managing your investment capital. For example, a trade with the risk-reward ratio of 1:4 shows that at the risk of $1, the trade has the potential of returning $4. Professional traders advise not to take any trade which has a risk-reward ratio lower than 1:3. This indicates, the trader can expect the investment to be $1, and the potential profit $3.

Expert traders use this method for planning which trade will be more profitable and take only those trades. Technical charting is a good technique to decide the risk-reward ratio of any trade by plotting the price moment from support to resistance levels. For example, if a stock has a support level at $20, it will probably rise from that level because many traders are likely to buy it at support levels. After finding out a potential support level, traders try to spot the nearby resistance level where the rising price is expected to pause. Suppose a technical level is appearing at $60. So, the trader can buy at $20 and exit when the price reaches $60. If everything goes right, he can risk $20 to reap a reward of $60. In this trade, the risk-reward ratio will be 1:3.

By calculating the risk-reward ratio, traders can plan how much money they will need to invest, and how much reward they can expect to gain from any trade. This makes them cautious about money management and risk management.

Some traders have a flexible risk-reward ratio for trading, while others prefer to take trades only with a fixed risk-reward ratio. Keeping stop-loss in all trades also helps in managing the risk-reward ratio. Traders can calculate their trade entry point to stop-loss as the risk, and trade entry to profit as the reward. This way, they can find out if any trade has a bigger risk than the potential reward or a bigger reward than the potential risk. Choosing trades with bigger profits and smaller risks can increase the amount of profit over a period.

Without learning money management, all your knowledge about stock and day trading is useless. If you don't use effective techniques for managing your investment, then you may soon find your money running out and you will have to shut down your day trading business. There are various methods for money management in intraday trading. It will be a good idea to learn a few techniques for it and strictly apply those rules to your trading business. Keeping the trading cost to a minimum and putting stop-loss in all trades are effective money management tricks.

Margin trading facilities are given for day trading and can be used astutely for increasing profits. At the same time, margin facilities can make day traders greedy, make them commit the mistake of over-trading, and incurring losses. Margin facility is borrowing money from your brokerage firm and trading on borrowed money is never a good idea. It is better to avoid margin trading until you have enough experience in stock markets and can handle your emotions while trading.

Day trading is not only profitable but can always lead to losses because of the ever-present market risk. Various events can trigger this risk and affect the performance of the overall stock markets. Day traders have no control over it. However, many strategies can help day traders avoid market risk, and reduce the potential loss that it can cause. Knowledge of stock markets' functioning and checking economic calendars can help day traders avoid some market risks.

Traders always face the risk of financial loss. Therefore, they must use strategies for risk management in day trading. Protecting your trading capital should be your first aim so you can stay in the day trading business for the long term. Creating trading plans and trading strategies are steps that can help traders avoid loss-making trades. Using stop orders is another method that can help traders reduce the losses and book their profits at the right time.

Calculating the risk-reward ratio is another method for money management and reducing risk trading. Traders can calculate how much risk a trade carries and how much potential profit it can earn for them. They can choose only those trades that carry a bigger reward and smaller risk and thus earn more profits in the long-term. Some professional traders prefer to trade only when the rewards are much higher than the potential risk.

Conclusion

Before you start trading, look around the market and make your plan on which combination of currencies will you trade. This depends on the volatility of their exchange prices, which is based on previous research done on the past profitable exchanges. Planning also includes the time that you are willing to sit down and monitor the trades, make sure that you stick to the time scheduled to avoid messing up the already earned profit. Remember that choosing the time to trade should be at a time when the market is more active. The market will be there tomorrow and, therefore, when your scheduled time arrives, close your trades. Strategy to be used throughout the

145

time you are trading should also be thought out before you start trading, and it should be adhered to throughout the trading period in the day.

When day trading, you have to know how to manage your money because at the end of the day you want to have money, not lose money. During the day, you will take part in several trades, and therefore you need to know the amount of money you will use to invest. You have to prepare for losses and gains, but the total loss you expect is of importance to avoid losing all your money at the end of the day. This starts by knowing the risk per trade; this is the amount of money you are ready to lose on one trade. If you are a beginner, it is good to set your risk at a maximum of 2%. The size of the account should also be taken into account. If you have a trade that according to you, has a stop-loss of close to 50 pips, if you risk $200, your risk will be $4. This is done by dividing the amount of money you are risking by the stop loss pips.

Always have a stop target before you start trading, and also consider the type of market you are trading in; some markets are so dynamic such that your stop order might not be executed as per the set value. Therefore, to be safe, set your stops using the actual price-action and the conditions prevailing in the market, it is good to set them around the resistance, and support levels, chart patterns, trend lines, and how volatile the currencies you are using are in the market. It is not only the stop loss position that you should consider during day trading, but also consider the point at which you want to take profits. For maximum profit, place appropriate levels of taking a profit.

Also, you should look at the reward-risk ratio, and when it is 1:1, it means that the amount you are risking equal to what you expect as a profit, and 3:1 has a triple amount to gain to lose. You can mix these trades such that you have many with a high potential of gaining and few with an equal potential of winning. You can do it the other way around, but make sure that there is a balance that will leave you with some profit.

Although trading takes place at all times in the world, each market region has its hours of trade. Therefore, as a trader, you should know your market, and it's opening and closing hours. You should also know that trading is not good throughout a trading day, and trading is good when the market activity is high. We have four major trading markets, and each of them has it is opening and closing hours. However, some markets open around the same time. For example,

Tokyo market open at 7 P.M and close at 4 A.M while the Sydney market opens at 5 P.M until 2 A.M looking at the opening hours of the two markets, there is a time when they are all open, and then, therefore, the level of activity with the currencies increases in the two markets between 5 P.M and 8 P.M when you are in the two markets, it is the best time to trade. This means that when more than one market is open at the same time, the trading activities are heightened, and the price of currencies fluctuates more. Therefore, maximize this by doing trades when the market is very active.

You should also be alert on any news release that can make the price of the currency to fluctuate as you look out for changes in prices. Remember that the news can go against the predicted trend, and if you had already taken a position, you can either lose or gain, and it happens in seconds. You can make money by reacting correctly and within the correct time in day trading. The news to look out for is the GDP data, trade deficits, central bank meetings and announcements, consumer confidence, among other big news affecting the economy in the region.

As you look out for the fluctuations in prices, stay in check not to open so many trades that you cannot control. Having many trades does not mean that you will get a lot of money. The best thing to do is to start your trade in small portions. Identify three trades that show potential and monitor the trends; it is good to deal with two trades in a day that you will maximize on their profits than dealing with many that you will not make money on.

The amount of money made in the day also depends on the type of trading strategy used. To make more money choose a trading system that will give you more. When using scalping, it can help you to gain more, but you should increase the number of trades because the income obtained from one trade is very small. This is done when your main strategy is scalping. You can do more than one hundred trades in a day so that at the end of the day you have many wins than losses thus at the end of the day you have good money in your wallet.

If you are doing scalping as a supplementary strategy, you should use it when the market is not giving a large range in terms of the fluctuation of prices of currencies. In this case, most of the time, there are no trends in a longer timeframe, and therefore using scalping in the short time frame becomes the best option to exploit. This way, you are assured that even without visible trends, there is a possibility that you will not end the day without money. This means that you initiate a long timeframe trade, and as it develops, you start new sets of trade with a shorter timeframe; it should be done in the same direction. You will then be entering and leaving the trade, as you collect small amounts, then later get a major profit with the long timeframe.

In a day, you can also use the false breakouts to make money in day trading. Looking at a trend, you can spot a breakout that you believe that it will not maintain the same direction. This is when you make a move, when the trend comes back to its original line; using this quick realization, you can make some cash. Using a fading breakout is the most effective because breakout tends to come out and out, and eventually, they succeed, but with a fading breakout, you will be sure of making money. The rationale of using breakouts is that the resistance and support levels are known as ceilings and price floors respectively, and when one of them is broken, traders expect the trend to continue in that direction and therefore, the traders react in the opposite direction, which later stabilizes the trend to its original flow. An example is that when the resistance level is broken, most traders think that the price will continue in the upward trend and buy the currency instead of selling. You should, therefore, sell the currency, acting contrary to what everyone is doing, and when the

150

breakout returns to normal, you buy again at a lower price. Similarly, when the support is broken, it means that the movement of the price is downwards, and most traders are likely to sell and not buy. To collect funds from this move, you should buy the currency instead of selling, and when the price resumes to its trend line, you sell it out. This type of trading is much profitable, but it can be very risky, therefore, analyze the graph well to make sure that it is a false breakdown before you enter the trade. However, to be safer, place a limit order when buying and selling, and make sure that at the end of the day, you have money in your wallet.

You can also make money using pivot points, which helps you to determine how prices of currencies are moving. Most of the time, the pivot points will identify prices as bullish or bearish, then represent the averages for the low, high prices and closing prices occurring on a trading day. Do you need to know the market trend? The pivot points will help you with that. Use the pivot points to determine the general direction of the trade; if the market price of the currency is above the base of the pivot point, it suggests that the trade is bullish, and when it is below the pivot base, then it is bearish. Also, when using pivot points, close all the long position trades when the market gets to the resistance levels and close the short ones when the market goes below the support level.

There is also the use of a reversal strategy that is commonly used around the globe; this strategy will help you to make money within a very short time, especially if the currency is moderately volatile. To use this strategy, you will have to study the graph to determine whether it has several consecutive highs and lows. At the highest point, which is called the top, you can easily predict that the price of the currency will reverse, and then react immediately by selling the currency. Similarly, if the graph of the currency has the lowest point, which is known as the bottoms, you predict that the trend will reverse, and buy the currency. When using this strategy, as long as you have predicted the reversal of the trend correctly, you will add money to your wallet.

In day trading, you are required to enter into many trades and exiting, depending on the type of strategy you are using. Therefore, to ensure that you have your funds available for trade when you need it, make sure that you focus on more liquid currencies. Remember that liquidity also comes with volatility. If you tie your money, you will get an opportunity and fail to utilize it because you have no funds at your disposal. Alternatively, always plan your trades such that your wallet does not get depleted because trading that is triggered by a news release is not planned, but when it arises, it is good to take advantage of the opportunity and to make quick money or take a position that will earn you more.

CPSIA information can be obtained
at www.ICGtesting.com
Printed in the USA
LVHW050530090221
678731LV00005B/134